D1394954

THE GLORY, GLORY BHOYS

THE GLORY GLORY BHOYS

The Celebration of Celtic's Triumphant
1997–98 Season

ANDY DOUGAN

MAINSTREAM
PUBLISHING

EDINBURGH AND LONDON

Copyright © Andy Dougan, 1998
All rights reserved
The moral right of the author has been asserted

First published in Great Britain in 1998 by
MAINSTREAM PUBLISHING COMPANY (EDINBURGH) LTD
7 Albany Street
Edinburgh EH1 3UG

ISBN 1 84018 155 9

No part of this book may be reproduced or transmitted in any form or by any
means without written permission from the publisher, except by a reviewer who
wishes to quote brief passages in connection with a review written for insertion in
a magazine, newspaper or broadcast

A catalogue record for this book is available from the British Library

Typeset in Times
Printed and bound in Great Britain by The Bath Press Ltd

To Christine, Iain and Stuart
and to the Glory, Glory Bhoys for a season to remember

ACKNOWLEDGEMENTS

I would like to thank a great many people at Celtic Park for their help and support in writing this book; especially to David Kells, Ray Turkington and Eleanor in the commercial department. I am also grateful to Peter McLean and his staff in the public relations department, especially Clare for whom nothing appeared to be too much trouble. My thanks also to the players – not just for winning the league – but also for offering their time and their memories. I am especially grateful to Jonathan Gould, Alan Stubbs and Tom Boyd who answered rather obvious questions with patience and good humour. Thanks also to Bill Campbell and Neil Graham at Mainstream and, as always, to my agent Jane Judd.

Above: *Darren Jackson, the first of the new faces*

Left: *Craig Burley's son Luke tries on the Hoops for size after his dad joins from Chelsea*

A BAD START

Hibs v Celtic
3 August 1997

The 1997–98 league campaign began for Celtic more in hope than expectation. The close season had been a difficult one with major changes in the management structure at Celtic Park. Manager Tommy Burns had left after three seasons which saw Celtic win only one trophy and – perhaps more significantly – consistently fail to beat Rangers in the league, which had allowed the Ibrox club to equal Celtic's record of nine league titles in a row. The old system of a team manager being responsible for everything had been ditched in favour of the Continental system of a head coach who would look after on-field matters and a general manager who would look after things off the field. Jock Brown, a lawyer who was best known as a TV commentator, was the new general manager, while Wim Jansen was the new coach. Jansen had played in the Feyenoord side which had beaten Celtic in the 1970 European Cup final and had also played in two World Cup finals for Holland. He had also coached with some success at Feyenoord but was still, as far as the Scottish media and most of the fans were concerned, an 'unknown'.

Jansen had joined his players on a pre-season tour of his native Holland and had been in charge of Celtic's first competitive games of the season in the UEFA Cup preliminary round. Celtic had won 8–0 but their opponents, Inter CableTel of Cardiff, were hardly a reasonable test of their abilities. His introduction to the Scottish Premier League came at Easter Road on Sunday, 3 August – Celtic were kicking off the season a day late because the game was being televised live. Hibs in their pomp were difficult opponents but, bearing in mind they had avoided relegation by a single game the previous season, they were not expected to provide too much resistance to Jansen's side.

Celtic took the field with two new faces. Former Hibs star Darren Jackson was making his league debut for Celtic having played and scored against CableTel, while Craig Burley, signed only a few days previously from Chelsea, was making his first appearance for his new club. Jackson and Burley were among a huge influx of new players who would arrive at Celtic Park in the first few weeks of the season as Jansen began to stamp his authority on the team. Many of them had been recommended by David Hay, who was steadily compiling a solid reputation for finding talent all across Europe.

Wim Jansen, the former Dutch World Cup star who would lead Celtic to glory

The appointment of Jansen would ultimately transform the way Celtic played football, but there was little sign of that at Easter Road. It was Hibs who surprised everyone by playing careful, controlled football and who took hold of the game right from the kick-off and never let go. The Celtic midfield was virtually non-existent. Burley, who seemed to be struggling from the sheer pace of the game, never exerted his influence, and the home side pretty much had things their own way – despite the fact that Darren Jackson looked to have achieved every player's dream in scoring against his old club until his ninth-minute 'goal' was deemed to be offside.

This was just about Celtic's only contribution to the game in the early part of the first half and, although the visiting fans may have been shocked, no one could really be surprised when Hibs went ahead in the twenty-third minute. Tony Rougier, who had previously been linked with Celtic under Tommy Burns, went down the left and was virtually unchallenged before firing a low cross into the Celtic penalty area. Despite having three Celtic defenders in close proximity, Lee Power had all the time in the world to slot the ball home under the onrushing Gordon Marshall.

Power's goal was something of a wake-up call for Celtic who shook themselves out of their lethargy and started to put some more consistent attacking moves together. A promising combination between Tommy Johnson and Darren Jackson in the twenty-seventh minute ended with

Hibs' new Icelandic keeper Olafur Gottskalksson making a good save. A minute later Celtic were back in the game. Their renewed pressure won them a corner on the left and, as Simon Donnelly swung the ball in, Malky Mackay managed to outjump two Hibs defenders to send a powerful header into the net, past a despairing attempt at a goal line clearance from a Hibs defender.

Both Mackay and Brian Welsh of Hibs required treatment for head injuries after their clash, but they were both able to continue. Celtic continued to press, but there were ominous signs that Hibs midfielder Chic Charnley was beginning to enjoy himself. Charnley had a long-cherished dream to play for Celtic and although he wore the Hoops once as a guest in a testimonial game, his dreadful disciplinary record had prevented the move of a lifetime. Nonetheless, he was having something of a purple patch in the green and white of Hibs and was tormenting the Celtic defence as the game wore on. Towards the end of the half he spotted Gordon Marshall out of his goal and attempted a daring 40-yard chip which was only denied by the crossbar.

Despite coming back into the game through Mackay's goal, Celtic

Simon Donnelly celebrates the equaliser in a pre-season friendly against Parma

were never able to get out of second gear and huffed and puffed to no great purpose. Johnson, Simon Donnelly and Darren Jackson all missed second-half chances, although Jackson can count himself unlucky to have one cleared off the line with the keeper beaten. Charnley, however, continued to be Celtic's chief tormentor in a second half which was going much the same way as the first. Jansen threw on another new boy, Henrik Larsson, for Andy Thom, in the hope that his pace would turn the game. Larsson was a bargain-buy from Feyenoord after a Dutch transfer tribunal found in Celtic's favour. The Swedish international did turn the game – but not in the way anyone would have hoped. With almost his first touch of the ball Larsson sent a slack clearance which found Charnley about 25 yards out. As Burley rushed to close him down, Charnley hit a screaming volley which sailed past Marshall and into the net which gave Hibs the lead once more.

The steal of the season – snatching Henrik Larsson for under £1 million

Charnley's goal was an accident waiting to happen as far as Celtic were concerned. Larsson's debut was one of the more ignominious of recent years, but he would very soon erase the memory of that first nightmare game. For Celtic, however, there were more horrors still to come.

Celtic 1	Hibs 2
Mackay	Power
	Charnley

Celtic: Marshall, Boyd, McKinlay, McNamara, Mackay, Stubbs, Donnelly, Burley, Johnson, Jackson, Thom

Substitutes: Larsson for Thom, Wieghorst for McKinlay

Bookings: Boyd, Burley

Attendance: 13,051

THE NIGHTMARE CONTINUES

Dunfermline v Celtic
16 August 1997

A strange quirk of the fixture list gave Celtic two weeks to stew over their dismal performance against Hibs. In between times they had a second-round Coca-Cola Cup tie against Berwick Rangers on 9 August. Berwick are best known for, perhaps, the most famous Cup upset in the history of Scottish football, when they beat Rangers in the Scottish Cup in 1967. After Celtic's performance against Hibs there were uncomfortable reminders of Berwick's giant-killing feat which could not be dismissed with a completely clear conscience.

The game against Berwick was being played at Tynecastle in order to accommodate the large crowd. Celtic fielded another two debutants: Jonathan Gould, who had been signed on a short-term deal from Bradford City in response to a goalkeeping crisis with Gordon Marshall and Stewart Kerr both having been injured; and Dutch winger Regi Blinker was signed from Sheffield Wednesday in a piece of transfer activity which saw unsettled winger Paulo Di Canio head for Hillsborough. Di Canio had been idolised by the Celtic Park faithful but claimed to have lost faith with the club after Tommy Burns' departure. Many fans were angry at the move and felt that more could have been done to keep the Italian at the club. Much of the fans' anger was directed at general manager Jock Brown for, as they saw it, not keeping them sufficiently well informed. The general manager insisted that the Blinker move and the Di Canio sale were two entirely separate pieces of business, nonetheless Brown would have to become used to being a public scapegoat for the club's perceived shortcomings in the months ahead. Stephane Mahé, a left-back who had been part of the Paris St Germain side which had demolished Celtic at Celtic Park two years previously, was another newish face in the side against Berwick.

Andy Thom opened Celtic's European account against Inter Cabletel

Mahé had been signed from Rennes and had made his Celtic debut in a mid-week friendly against Roma which Celtic won 1–0. The Coca-Cola Cup tie would be his first competitive game.

All thoughts of giant-killing evaporated as Celtic beat Berwick 7–0 with a debut goal from Blinker, who was joined on the score-sheet by Wieghorst, Larsson, Jackson, Thom and Donnelly (2). The going was somewhat harder in Austria a few days later when Celtic met SC Tirol in the second qualifying round of the UEFA Cup. Once again Celtic struggled and found themselves two-nil down, until a late goal from Alan Stubbs gave them some hope of going through in the home leg.

Nonetheless, a midweek European trip and a 2–1 defeat were not the ideal preparations for Celtic's second league game of the season. In their favour their opponents were Dunfermline, who should be well within Celtic's compass and, since it was their first home game of the season, they could also count on the passionate support of some 47,000 fans. The Celtic side that day featured a handful of new Bhoys as five players – Jonathan Gould, Henrik Larsson, Craig Burley, Darren Jackson and Regi Blinker – made their Celtic Park league debuts.

The new faces were given a rapturous reception and Celtic began the game as they had finished the previous season. Wave after wave of attack beat down upon the Dunfermline goal, and keeper Ian Westwater was one of the busiest men on the park as he marshalled his defence to deal with the Celtic threat. Wim Jansen was modifying Celtic's style from the traditional cavalry charge to a more studied, but still lightning-quick, break from back to front. Possession was the key and although Celtic had a lot of the ball they were still having difficulty in converting this into goals. In the first half alone they forced nine corners, with Blinker spending most of the half trotting from flag to flag, though with no great effect. This would be a hallmark of Celtic's play throughout the season and for all

The backroom team: David Hay, Murdo MacLeod, John Clark and general manager Jock Brown

the use they made of their corners they would have been as well not taking them at all.

Larsson, Blinker, Jackson and Thom poured forward, but Dunfermline managed to keep the scoresheet clean with a mixture of luck, desperation and resolute defending. Finally the pressure told on Dunfermline. In the thirty-ninth minute Blinker put Larsson clear, as he had done so often in the half. Again, as had happened so often, Westwater seemed to be in a good position but, unaccountably, veteran defender Hamish French stepped in and obstructed Larsson. Andreas Thom stepped up to take the penalty-kick and sent Westwater diving to his right while the ball went in at the left-hand post. On balance Celtic deserved their half-time lead and the capacity crowd looked forward to more of the same in the second half, now that the nerves had settled.

The second half started with both teams on the pitch but mentally Celtic were plainly still in the dressing-room. As the fans streamed back from their half-time pies and Bovril they found their half-time lead had gone. A weak clearance from Tosh McKinlay was picked up by Alan Moore, who was able to run unopposed into the Celtic box before releasing a well-timed pass to John Bingham. Although there were three Celtic defenders in the penalty area, Bingham had all the time in the world to control the ball and, as Jackie McNamara made a despairing sliding tackle, fire it past a helpless Jonathan Gould.

What should have been a triumphant procession became a horror story for Celtic. Once again the midfield failed to take control of the game, allowing Dunfermline to come more and more into the match. The quick passing and controlled possession of the first half from Celtic degenerated into painful Route One football as the ball was hoicked up the park at every opportunity. When Wim Jansen took over at Celtic the received wisdom was that he was mild mannered and amiable. There was no sign of that as Jansen stood furiously on the edge of the tactical area outside his dug-out, with his arms flung wide like a demented angler, as he tried to encourage his team to attack down the flanks. Despite his frantic exhortation there was no one to take charge and, just as had happened at Easter Road two weeks earlier, Celtic found themselves chasing the game. Dunfermline, who would probably have bitten the hand of anyone who had offered them a point from Celtic Park at the start of the game, now began to capitalise on Celtic's disarray. The game was there for the taking and, in the seventy-seventh minute, Alan Moore was again the architect of Celtic's downfall. He was pulled down by Mackay as he broke through in the penalty box and the referee had no hesitation in giving the penalty. French, who had conceded the penalty which put Celtic ahead, made no mistake in atoning for his sins. He coolly placed the ball into the same corner in which Andy Thom had scored in the first half, with Gould nowhere near it.

Celtic had no answer and managed to hold on until the final whistle without Dunfermline inflicting further damage, thanks mainly to a great save from Gould which prevented a third goal. McKinlay had had a thoroughly miserable day at the office. The players walked off the field like condemned men with the boos and jeers of those fans who had remained ringing in their ears. After two games Celtic were at the bottom of the league without a single point.

Celtic 1	Dunfermline 2
Thom, pen	Bingham
	French, pen

Celtic: Gould, Boyd, McKinlay, McNamara, Mackay, Hannah, Larsson, Burley, Jackson, Thom, Blinker

Substitutes: Donnelly for Thom, O'Donnell for McKinlay

Bookings: Mackay, Blinker

Attendance: 46,206

SAVED!

St Johnstone v Celtic
23 August 1997

One strange aspect of Celtic's progress in the Coca-Cola Cup in 1997 was the number of times they would have to play what amounted to 'double-headers', with two games against the same team inside a matter of days. The first of these was against St Johnstone, who Celtic were drawn against in the third round of the Coca-Cola Cup only four days before they were due to meet them in the league. Both games were to be played at McDiarmid Park in Perth. Popular wisdom has it that either of the Old Firm is never more than three games away from a crisis but, given the start that Celtic had made to the season, if the theory held true then they were now just 90 minutes away from the jaws of disaster.

Another defeat would be unthinkable, which may account for the style of game which Celtic adopted in the Coca-Cola Cup. Possession was paramount. Wim Jansen and his players had held a 'clear-the-air' session after the Dunfermline game, in which there was a full and frank exchange of views on both sides. It seems that the players had misunderstood Jansen's instructions about the type of game he wanted them to play.

'When we used to train he used to say he wanted the ball forward as quickly as possible,' explains Alan Stubbs. 'So we changed our formation and we were playing three at the back, five in midfield and two at the front, with one from midfield always pushing forward. We were getting the impression that whenever we got it, he just wanted the ball to the wide areas as quick as possible, and to the forwards as quick as possible. We were all looking at each other and going: "We don't want to play this way. It's not us and it's not the way we wanted to play." As players we'd had enough and we were disillusioned and we asked for the meeting. I think he was glad really because it meant he could explain to us what he meant.

'We had the meeting and, at the end of the day, it was just a case of crossed wires. It wasn't that he wanted us to play a long ball, it was just that whenever we got it he wanted us to get it wide early, not just lump it. He wanted us to get forward early, so we might catch the other team off-guard and not make so many square passes. Once we had our meeting we didn't really look back, everything was clear. There were no harsh words, it was a professional meeting in which we expressed what we felt and he expressed what he felt. It was a very amicable session.'

The results of this collective heart-to-heart were immediately apparent. Against St Johnstone, Celtic looked a much more fluid side – but there was still a nervousness about their play. There was lots of possession, but nothing which could be converted into real chances, and St Johnstone looked as likely to score as Celtic. In the end it was all-square after 90 minutes and Celtic rode their luck in extra-time.

The new Bhoys: Craig Burley, Stephane Mahe, Henrik Larsson and Darren Jackson

Celtic's first stroke of luck came in 99 minutes when John O'Neil of St Johnstone was involved in a tackle which left Stephane Mahé on the ground. As Malky Mackay approached the pair of them, O'Neil lashed out and kicked the air, apparently in frustration. Referee Hugh Dallas, however, felt there was intent in his actions – even though he might have been the only man in the ground who thought so – and O'Neil was sent off. Six minutes later Celtic won a softish penalty when the ball bounced off the turf and made contact with Callum Davidson's hand. Whether Davidson handled the ball or the ball hit Davidson is open to conjecture. What is not in doubt is that contact was made and the referee awarded a penalty which Simon Donnelly converted for the only goal of the game. St Johnstone, in fact, finished the game with nine men after Roddy Grant was sent off for deliberately handling the ball in the dying moments.

The midweek win certainly put Celtic in a better frame of mind going into the Saturday game at McDiarmid Park. There was still no disguising the fact that another bad result could leave them in desperate straits. Defeat in the league could leave them nine points adrift of Rangers, with the first Old Firm game of the season only a week away. There were, however, distinct signs of change in the way Celtic were playing. Now that the breakdown in communications had been rectified, Celtic were starting to play as a cohesive unit. Craig Burley was beginning to take a real grip of the midfield along with a rejuvenated Morten Wieghorst. The Danish international seemed to have slipped out of Tommy Burns' thinking through a combination of poor form and injury. Under Jansen he had found a new lease of life and acquired the confidence to make surging runs out of the midfield. But the key to the 'new' Celtic was Henrik Larsson. The dreadlocked Swede was the epitome of the Jansen philosophy. He used the ball intelligently, gathering it in the middle of the park, laying it off and then using his blistering pace to find a gap in the defence. The ball could then be played back to Larsson to either take a shot himself, or hold the ball until others came forward in support.

The travelling Celtic fans had to wait a long time for the opening goal in this game, but when it came, just a minute before half-time, it was a text-book example of how goals would be scored by this Celtic side. Craig Burley gathered the ball deep in his own half and slipped it to Larsson at the edge of the centre circle. The Swedish international carried it into the St Johnstone half before laying it off to Donnelly, who was playing wide on the right. Donnelly jogged forward before sending a deadly accurate cross into the box allowing Larsson, who had continued his run, to throw himself full length and head past Alan Main. It was a goal which was magnificent in its simplicity and there was more to come. Indeed only seconds later an effort from Blinker careened off the Saints crossbar.

Celtic went in at half-time well worth their lead but, although they had dominated the game, they would also have been well aware that they owed their dominance to goalkeeper Jonathan Gould. St Johnstone were encouraged by the fact that they had only lost to Celtic by a single goal over 120 minutes in the midweek game and that George O'Boyle had

Jonathan Gould, snapped up from Bradford, ended his season at the World Cup

already had the ball in the net in the ninth minute, but was ruled offside. Twenty-five minutes later, O'Boyle found himself clear with the ball at his feet with no question of offside. The Celtic defence had been dragged out of position over on the right and were left flat-footed when the ball was whipped across to O'Boyle. He was eight yards out and on his own when he let fly with a fearsome volley. The Saints fans were already out of their seats when Gould leaped to his left, twisting to pluck the ball from behind him and turning it onto the post before Mahé could hook it to safety.

Looking back on what was one of the pivotal moments in Celtic's season, Gould was well aware of the importance of the save but also insisted that it was simply a case of a goalkeeper doing what he's paid to do.

'I remember turning to face O'Boyle but I think it was purely a reaction save,' he recalls. 'Goalkeepers will tell you that a lot of the saves they make are instinctive. All I can remember is that the boy on the wide-right pinged the ball across the box and the next thing I knew was O'Boyle shaping up to volley it. I think I was basically moving my feet across to get in line with him and he fired the shot and it hit me on the hand and it was away. I think I knew it was vital that it stayed at 0–0 and we needed something to kick-start the season, then, fortunately, Henrik got up the other end and scored with a diving header.'

Bolstered by Gould's efforts Celtic swept forward and eventually took the lead in 44 minutes. In the second half, just on the hour mark, Celtic once again turned dogged defence into venomous attack with one seamless move. This time it was Wieghorst who picked up a loose ball out of the Saints defence. Without so much as looking up, the Dane sent the ball immediately to Darren Jackson. The former Hibs star easily evaded a tackle from Jim Weir, looked up briefly, and then rifled a curling shot into the top of the net. Alan Main managed to get a hand to it, but it was not enough to stop Jackson scoring his first league goal for Celtic.

With two goals in the bag and half an hour still to play, Celtic were coasting. They were finally starting to click as a unit. Larsson was having his best game to date in a hooped shirt and he constantly tormented the St Johnstone defence. Jackson came close as well and Burley had one cannon off the crossbar.

Finally the fans had something to sing about. The long climb up the league had begun.

Celtic 2   St Johnstone 0
Larsson
Jackson

Celtic: Gould, Boyd, Mahé, Hannah, Mackay, Wieghorst, Larsson, Burley, Donnelly, Jackson, Blinker

Substitutes: O'Donnell for Blinker

Bookings: Larsson, Blinker

Attendance: 10,265

JUST A GAME

Motherwell v Celtic
10 September 1997

There are those who believe that football isn't a matter of life and death; it's more important than that. But it is only a game, albeit the greatest game in the world, but only a game for all that. The events of the last week in August summed up for Celtic fans that there is more to life than just football.

Encouraged by their back-to-back victories over St Johnstone and with that vital away goal from Alan Stubbs to their credit, Celtic went into the return leg of their UEFA Cup tie against SC Tirol with some confidence. There had been some speculation about Jansen's team selection beforehand. Would the injured Stubbs be back for this fixture? Would McNamara, another casualty of the Dunfermline game, be able to wrest his place back from David Hannah? In the end there was no place in the starting line-up for either Stubbs or McNamara, but the Celtic Park fans were genuinely astonished not to hear Darren Jackson's name in the final 11, or among the five substitutes. Nonetheless, with a game to be won against decent opposition who had a goal of a start, the 47,000 crowd buckled down to the task of cheering on the team. European nights at Celtic Park are always electrifying events and very soon it was business as usual.

Celtic started confidently but patiently and it took 33 minutes before they broke down a disciplined Austrian defence. Eventually it was Wieghorst who found Donnelly with a perfectly weighted chip which the young striker volleyed home. It was now 2–2 on aggregate, with Celtic having the advantage of that away goal. The delight of the crowd did not last long. Within five minutes Tirol's star player, and Celtic's chief tormentor, Christian Mayrleb, ran onto a neat pass and scored for the Austrians – making it 1–1 on the night and 3–2 to Tirol on

Simon Donnelly scores from the spot in the 6–3 win against FC Tirol

aggregate. It was then the turn of Henrik Larsson to play hero and villain within the space of a few minutes. First he was involved in a free-kick move with Andreas Thom, which led to Thom restoring Celtic's lead with a fierce shot which went in off the post. Then Larsson managed to get in the way of a wicked cross from Mayrleb and, somewhat unfortunately, turn the ball into his own net. At half-time it was 2–2 on the night with the Austrians leading 4–3 on aggregate, and, more significantly, they had now scored more away goals than Celtic, which would give them the advantage if the tie ended as a draw on aggregate.

By the standards of the first half, the second 45 minutes started quietly with Celtic putting the Austrians under pressure without adding to their total. In the sixty-eighth minute, however, Larsson, who had been tormenting the Tirol defence for most of the night, was pulled down inside the box and Donnelly coolly scored from the penalty spot. Two minutes later it was Larsson again who left a trio of Austrian defenders in his wake before slipping the ball to Burley, who scored his first goal for Celtic with a fierce shot. With 20 minutes of the tie left Celtic were ahead for the first time; 4–2 on the night and 5–4 on aggregate. The atmosphere on the terracing was approaching hysteria, this was not the best European tie Celtic Park had seen by a long way, but it was certainly a contender for the most exciting. And there was more to come.

Tirol had always fancied themselves sneaking the tie and in the eighty-first minute they looked to have done that. Substitute Krinner had only been on the park a matter of seconds when he scored a third for the Austrians with a header that was virtually his first touch of the ball. Time was running out for Celtic but, urged on by the raucous screaming of 47,000 raw throats, they were still in the game. Three minutes from the end Wieghorst put them back in front on aggregate with a simple but well-taken strike, then, in the ninetieth minute Burley, again set up by Larsson, scored a sixth for Celtic. It was 6–3 on the night, 7–5 on aggregate and although the referee inexplicably added five minutes of extra time on to the second half – just as he had with the first – Celtic were through to the next round.

Within 24 hours the euphoria of the players and the fans was put into perspective when details of Darren Jackson's absence from the side came to light. The striker had complained of a headache on the morning of the game and taken some painkillers. The pain persisted and on the coach up from Seamill to Celtic Park he complained of feeling unwell. Team doctor Dr Jack Mulhearn examined him at the ground and said there was no way that Jackson could play. Dr Mulhearn knew that Jackson was not prone to headaches and was concerned about their severity and persistence. He decided that the player should have a brain scan and, after further tests, it was revealed that Jackson had hydrocephalus, a condition which causes a build up of pressure in the brain and hence blinding headaches. Although not immediately life-threatening it would require surgery if Jackson was ever to contemplate playing football again. By the end of the week the striker was preparing to go under the knife.

The news of Jackson's illness was a blow to everyone at Celtic Park but, as messages of support and goodwill flooded in from all over the world, they had no option but to put this all behind them and try to prepare for their first meeting of the season with Rangers. Fortunately, the game had been switched from the usual Saturday until Monday night, which gave the Celtic squad some much needed time to recover from the exertions of the Tirol game. However, on the following Sunday – the day before the game – Diana, Princess of Wales was killed in a car crash in Paris. Given the circumstances, there was no way a game as potentially volatile as an Old Firm fixture could go ahead with the country unofficially in mourning. The game was rescheduled for 19 November which would mean Celtic and Rangers would meet in the league twice in the space of 11 days. A few days later the Celtic players and officials were dealt another blow with the news that former Celt Brian Whittaker had been killed in a car crash, at the age of 40.

It is just a game after all.

The postponement of the Rangers game and a blank week because of Scotland's World Cup commitments meant that Celtic had almost a fortnight between the European tie against Tirol and their next game. In between times, two other off-field events exercised the minds of Celtic fans. The first was the eventual transfer of striker Jorge Cadete to Celta Vigo for £3 million. Cadete is without doubt the best six-yard-box striker Celtic had seen in years, but personal problems had kept him at home in Portugal since the close season. His departure meant he was the last of the trio of disaffected foreigners – the others were DiCanio and Dutchman Pierre van Hooijdonk – to discover 'small problems' with their contracts after reviving their careers at Celtic. The second piece of off-field news was a good deal more exciting. After beating Tirol, Celtic had been rewarded with a tie against old enemies Liverpool in the next round. The prospect of this tie was absolutely mouth-watering, but before then, it was back to 'auld claes and porridge' as they concentrated on domestic affairs.

Stephane Mahe quickly found his feet on the left side of the Celtic defence

The Coca-Cola Cup quarter-final against Motherwell on 10 September was another of those double-headers, since the two sides were due to meet in the league on 13 September. The two-week break and the news that Darren Jackson was on his way back to a full recovery lifted whatever gloom may have been hanging around Celtic Park. The first tie against Motherwell was perhaps the best Celtic had played all season. It's fair to say that Celtic murdered them 1–0.

Larsson was again the architect of the victory. Thom, Donnelly, Boyd, Burley, it seemed everyone except Jonathan Gould had a crack at the Motherwell goal which survived intact by good luck and fine goalkeeping. Donnelly had a goal disallowed, Motherwell keeper Woods then pushed another shot onto the bar and managed to grab the rebound and then Woods made an inspired save from Burley to deny the midfielder. The breakthrough came initially from Stephane Mahé. As the season wore on the Frenchman would become more and more confident with his forays down the left. This early transition to attacking mode saw Mahé send a fierce cross raking in at the near post with Larsson perfectly positioned for the header past Woods and the despairing Brian Martin.

Celtic's dominance could be seen from the fact that Motherwell didn't have a shot on goal until the seventieth minute. But when they did, Celtic's defensive frailties almost cost them the game. Not for the first time in the season Jonathan Gould was called on to make two great saves to defend the result.

'The art of being a goalkeeper with Celtic is to remain switched on at all times,' Gould explains. 'A lot of the possession goes with us at home and you have to make sure at all times that you're aware that something could be required of you. I might not appear to be a screamer but I can assure you I am and I think I stay focused by keeping communication with the back four. I think there comes a time, maybe in the last third of the pitch, when I do then switch on to my job instead of what the other boys are doing.'

Having beaten them comfortably at home in the Coca-Cola Cup, Celtic were now looking forward to more of the same when, four days later, they went to Fir Park in the league. There was another new face in the Celtic side for the Motherwell game. The club had finally signed long-time transfer target Marc Rieper from West Ham on the Friday and the experienced Danish international made his debut against Motherwell the following day. Rieper had been bought to mesh with Alan Stubbs as twin centre-halves in Wim Jansen's radical reconstruction of the Celtic defence. Ironically, while Rieper never put a foot wrong, it was Stubbs who gifted Motherwell an opening goal when Coyne ran on to a short back pass with only three minutes gone.

Craig Burley celebrates his first Celtic goal, against Motherwell at Fir Park

Simon Donnelly clinches the points against Motherwell with a seemingly impossible header

In contrast to the midweek fixture this was an ugly ill-tempered affair, but again Celtic did all of the pressing. It took until the fifty-seventh minute for an equaliser, when Burley turned in a Larsson cross. However, within two minutes Motherwell were back in front: former Celt Tommy Coyne scoring his second goal of the game. Not long after, Motherwell had Greg Denham sent off for a second bookable offence in a game which saw nine yellow cards altogether. Celtic made the extra man tell and, in 76 minutes, Stubbs atoned for his sins with a perfectly judged pass to Burley which the midfielder then fired home from long range. Celtic continued to press and in 82 minutes Simon Donnelly made an acrobatic leap to head home a McNamara cross which appeared to have gone behind him.

The win against Motherwell finally put Celtic's goal-difference column into the black and – after two wins and two losses from four games – they were now sitting mid-table, four points behind leaders Hibs with a game in hand.

And looming on the horizon were the red shirts of Liverpool.

Celtic 3   Motherwell 2
Burley (2)   Coyne
Donnelly

Celtic: Gould, Boyd, Rieper, Stubbs, Mahé, Thom, Burley, Wieghorst, Blinker, Donnelly, Larsson

Substitutes: McNamara for Thom

Bookings: Burley, Wieghorst, Larsson

Attendance: 11,550

YOU'LL NEVER WALK ALONE

Aberdeen v Celtic
20 September 1997

The reason why one of the great Broadway show tunes should have become one of the great football anthems is shrouded in the mists of time. Whatever it is there is no doubt that Richard Rodgers and Oscar Hammerstein would never have heard a version of any of their songs to match the one at Celtic Park on 16 September 1997. A shade under 50,000 fans joined together in a chorus of 'You'll Never Walk Alone' possessed of such sheer primal majesty as to make the hairs on the back of your neck prickle with excitement.

Celtic were playing Liverpool in the first-round proper of the UEFA Cup. Having dispensed with CableTel and SC Tirol this was the big one. The zonal nature of the UEFA draw had made it likely that Celtic would be drawn against a big name, but this was a draw to set the pulse racing. The two teams have a long and distinguished relationship which goes back to the turn of the century. They have regularly called on the services of the other for testimonials to long-serving players and officials – Tommy Burns, Ian Rush, Jock Stein, Billy McNeill and Ron Yeats have all marked their testimonials with games between the two clubs. Such is the closeness of the relationship that it was Celtic who provided the opposition in a charity game at Celtic Park to benefit the victims of the Hillsborough disaster only two weeks after one of the blackest days in football history. Yet, although they had met 14 times over the years there had been only one competitive meeting between the clubs until now.

In 1966 Celtic had been drawn against Liverpool in the semi-final of the European Cup-Winners' Cup. Celtic all but destroyed them in the first game at Celtic Park, but so many chances were spurned they had only a 1–0 lead to take to Anfield. Liverpool were 2–0 ahead in the second leg but, with minutes to go, Bobby Lennox scored a great goal which would have given Celtic the tie on the away-goals rule. Or at least he thought he had. The goal was disallowed for offside, even though the referee was patently wrong, and Lennox to this day insists he was robbed. Since 1966 the fortunes of both clubs have fluctuated but as they went into this UEFA Cup tie Liverpool were clear favourites.

The Anfield side was brimming with major international names such as Karl-Heinz Reidle, Paul Ince and Steve McManaman. The good news for Celtic was that Liverpool striker Robbie Fowler was unfit, the bad news was that teen prodigy Michael Owen was in the side. Celtic came onto the field apparently overawed by the prospect of playing the

Henrik Larsson gets the better of Liverpool's Bjorn Tore Kvarme in the 2–2 game at Parkhead

might of Liverpool. Within five minutes it was Owen who had put Liverpool ahead, as he raced on to a pass from Reidle and chipped the ball over Gould. Celtic had no reply as Liverpool toyed with them in the middle of the park. It was more than 20 minutes before Celtic launched their first attack and when they did they could see that Jansen's exhortations of 'wider, wider' were paying off. There were times when it seemed that Jansen would not be happy until one winger was in Duke Street and the other in London Road, but there was no doubt that Liverpool could be stretched. Celtic took heart from this and suddenly realised they were playing the men and not the jerseys. Despite the loss of Blinker – who was stretchered off in 46 minutes after a heavy challenge from Rob Jones – Celtic were back in the game.

Regi Blinker eventually went off with a dislocated shoulder after several bruising encounters with the Liverpool defence

In 53 minutes McNamara collected a one-two from Burley and lashed a volley past the helpless David James. Then in 73 minutes Celtic were awarded a penalty when James brought down Larsson as the striker rounded him. It was a soft award but Larsson had seemed certain to score. In any event Simon Donnelly once again showed his composure by scoring from the spot to put Celtic in front.

Celtic seemed to have done enough to ensure a famous European victory. But, in 89 minutes, with the crowd whistling for full time, Steve McManaman picked up the ball inside his own half before setting off on a 45-yard run which evaded three Celtic defenders and ended up with a curling shot which beat Gould and came in off the far post. Liverpool had got out of jail with what turned out to be one of the goals of the season.

The game against Liverpool at Celtic Park, and the subsequent

Simon Donnelly comes close with a first-half shot against Liverpool

return leg at Anfield, would be significant turning points in Celtic's season. Having taken a team like Liverpool to within 60 seconds of a memorable result there was a new-found confidence running through a Celtic side which was now starting to gel as a unit. The addition of Marc Rieper – even though he had signed too late to play against Liverpool – meant the regular back four of Boyd, Rieper, Stubbs and Mahé was turning into a formidable defensive unit. But it was the conversion of a former defender which really played a key part in changing the way Celtic played. Jackie McNamara had been bought from Dunfermline as a right-back and, although he was impressive, he was never quite the finished article. Wim Jansen certainly thought so. To put it

Another new face: Marc Rieper made his debut against Motherwell only hours after signing from West Ham

bluntly he didn't much fancy McNamara as a full back. McNamara was left out of the side after the Dunfermline defeat and was finding it difficult to get back into the team. On sheer instinct and perhaps influenced by his belief that Liverpool could be stretched, Jansen decided to play McNamara against Liverpool – but not in defence. Jansen converted McNamara into an attacking midfielder, using him almost as a right-winger, and the results were immediate. Celtic now had more attacking options from the midfield, they had a player who could link with Larsson who was playing further forward than he preferred, and they had a wing-back who could pressurise the opposing full back.

The balance that McNamara brought to the Celtic side was seen almost immediately in their next game, against Aberdeen at Celtic Park. Aberdeen were a shadow of their former selves, but could usually be counted on to raise their game against Celtic. The truth is they were demolished by a display of free-running football which had not been seen at Celtic Park for some time. Once again it was Larsson who did the damage, scoring two goals to mark his twenty-sixth birthday. But the all round quality of Celtic's performance was simply breathtaking. Andreas Thom had one of his finest 90 minutes for Celtic in a rare full game. His diagonal runs and quick passing tormented the Aberdeen defence for most of the game. But, despite Thom in full flight, this was Larsson's day. In 27 minutes he took a ball from Simon Donnelly out on the right to glide between keeper Jim Leighton and defender David Rowson to score. Then, in the thirty-ninth minute, the Swede struck a beautiful free-kick from 20 yards out, which flew over the wall and into the net. Aberdeen were never really in the game and Celtic, with the game well under control, could afford to take their foot off the pedal.

The victory against Aberdeen was the end of a big week for Celtic, and one which would go a long way to setting them up for the rest of the season.

Celtic 2   Aberdeen 0
Larsson 2

Celtic: Gould, Boyd, Mahé, McNamara, Rieper, Stubbs, Larsson, Burley, Donnelly, Thom, Wieghorst

Substitutes: Hannah for Stubbs, O'Donnell for McNamara

Bookings: None

Attendance: 49,017

A NEW HOPE

Dundee United v Celtic
27 September 1997

Wim Jansen had been a late arrival at Celtic Park. He had joined the club only days before the start of the season and only met up with his players on their pre-season tour. On top of that he had now introduced seven new faces – Jackson, Gould, Burley, Larsson, Mahé, Blinker and Rieper – into his squad. Things had started disastrously for him but they were slowly and surely improving to the point where, when they played as they did against Aberdeen, Celtic were playing some of the most attractive football in the country. This had always been a hallmark of any worthwhile Celtic side, but Jansen had added a new dimension. Celtic were playing in a more Continental style and, instead of sweeping forward recklessly at the sound of the bugles, they were more intent on keeping possession.

Although he would be hailed, somewhat extravagantly, as a Celtic legend by the end of the season, Jansen did not enjoy unanimous support from the terraces in the early days. The fans who had been raised on the cavalry charge took a long time to get used to seeing Celtic players knocking the ball around in their own half and building patiently from the back. They also found it a little hard to take to the notion that, as against Aberdeen, if you go two goals up by half-time there is little need to add to that in the second half. Celtic had been more than capable of squandering two-goal leads in the past but now, under Jansen, once Celtic went two ahead the game was finished. Jansen had rebuilt the Celtic defence into a formidable unit and at the heart of that unit was the partnership between Alan Stubbs and Marc Rieper. Stubbs had been a big-money signing from Bolton just before the 1997–98 season but had never quite lived up to his billing. In his first season he had been sent off on his league debut and endured a run

After almost eight months at Celtic, a relieved David Hannah bags his first goal in the home tie against Inter Cabletel

of poor form and injury which all contributed to a thoroughly miserable season. Now Stubbs was a changed player. He was rock-solid in defence, marshalling those around him, and also able to ping 60-yard passes from the back. Stubbs became a linchpin in converting redoubtable defence to stinging attack with a single pass. Fans were to become used to seeing the ball leave Stubbs and drop neatly into the path of the onrushing Henrik Larsson.

'I think when I first came to Celtic it was a difficult year for a number of reasons,' Stubbs explains looking back on his first season. 'It was my first big move, I had just been married, my wife had a baby and it was a question of coming to a club where expectations were a lot higher and everything just seemed to be rolled into one. It was a matter of having to deal with it and I couldn't really. I needed time to settle down and, unfortunately, it took me longer than I wanted. Last year I proved to everyone what I can do and why the club spent a lot of money on me. When Marc came it was reassuring that I could go forward and not worry about what was behind me, whereas when I first came here it was the total opposite.'

The signing of Marc Rieper was a master stroke. Rieper was impressive in the air, unflinching in the tackle and able to use the ball once he had won it. Operating as twin centre-halves, Rieper and Stubbs could defend together and then break forward into attack without leaving the back door open.

'The understanding is that because I'm the spare man most of the time I can go into the hole in front of us when the midfielders need help,' Stubbs explains. 'Marc is usually picking up, which gives me a licence to go forward whenever I want and that suits me fine. Marc has his attributes and I've got mine and we know what they are and I think they work quite well together.'

Like Celtic, Dundee United had made a thoroughly miserable start to the season. Unlike Celtic, they had not been able to turn it around. When the teams met at Tannadice, United were still without a single win and had managed only three draws from their first five games. Nonetheless, the trip to Tannadice was perceived as a serious test of the mini-revival which Celtic had put together in the past few weeks. Although they had not had the results, United were deemed capable of raising their game sufficiently to put Celtic under pressure.

Injury to Stephane Mahé forced Jansen to reorganise his defence for the United game. But the Frenchman's place was not taken by Tosh McKinlay. Rather than use the out-of-favour McKinlay, Jansen went with David Hannah coming into the defence at right-back along with Boyd – who had switched to the left – Rieper and Stubbs. However, Jansen persisted with Jackie McNamara in the attacking midfield role which he had taken since the Liverpool game.

As expected, United did make things difficult for Celtic. This game turned into a test of character more than anything

The understanding between Simon Donnelly and Jackie McNamara was starting to pay dividends

Simon Donnelly scores against Dundee United with keeper Dykstra well beaten

Larsson and McNamara help Donnelly celebrate his opener in the 2–1 win at Tannadice.

Phil O'Donnell scores Celtic's second to take all three points

else, and there wasn't much in the way of flowing football. It was a game in which Celtic had to practise the virtues which Jansen had tried to instil into them; keep your shape, keep possession and don't chase the game. Even though it was not the most attractive game of the season, right from the start there were signs that United didn't stand a chance. The Tannadice defence had no reply to the direct running of Larsson and McNamara. Pressley, in particular, was like a rabbit frozen in the headlights every time Larsson ran at him. At the back Stubbs had a particularly effective game and the anticipated threat from United's Robbie Winters never materialised.

It was McNamara in his new-found attacking role who was the key to the Celtic performance. In 28 minutes he sent a long ball forward, which bounced in front of Pressley. The United defender had been having a torrid time and, with Larsson running at him from one side and Donnelly from the other, he should have dealt with the ball more quickly. Instead, he allowed it to bounce, Larsson beat him to it and flipped a neat header across to Donnelly who headed past Dykstra and into the net. The goal spurred Celtic into a period of intense pressure as they continued to dominate. Donnelly went close again with a shot that was only stopped by Dykstra's legs, McNamara had one cleared off the line and Stubbs went close with a free-kick. The second goal was always going to come and it came just before half-time. Jansen had brought on Phil O'Donnell for Andreas Thom in 41 minutes and with his first touch of the ball O'Donnell put Celtic two ahead. Again it was McNamara who did the damage with a long crossfield ball after United had lost possession in their own half. The ball sailed over the defence and into the path of O'Donnell who volleyed it left-footed into the net.

Celtic went in two-nil up but there was more resistance from United in the second half. Jonathan Gould was a little busier as Swedish striker Kjell Olofsson began to cause some problems. United got one back in the sixty-first minute from an Olofsson free-kick, but the Celtic defence stood firm. Rieper and Stubbs were there to pick up the threat before United could get too close and, indeed, in the closing minutes it was Celtic who looked more like scoring as Donnelly and Burley missed chances.

It was a good win for Celtic – who had now won eight of their last nine games. The only blemish was that draw against Liverpool and with the return leg in only four days, Celtic were in good heart.

Celtic 2	Dundee United 1
Donnelly	Olofsson
O'Donnell	

Celtic: Gould, Hannah, Rieper, Stubbs, Boyd, McNamara, Burley, Wieghorst, Thom, Larsson, Donnelly

Substitutes: O'Donnell for Thom, McKinlay for Wieghorst

Bookings: Burley, Wieghorst

Attendance: 11,367

TEN IN A ROW

Kilmarnock v Celtic
4 October 1997

The second half of the first leg of the UEFA Cup tie against Liverpool at Celtic Park had defined Celtic's season so far. They had come back from a goal down, dominated one of the best sides in Europe and had only had victory plucked from their grasp by an equaliser that would be one of the goals of the season. The confidence they gained from that spell of play would sustain them through the season and, together with an unbeaten run of nine games, they should have been going to Anfield in good heart for the return on 30 September. But there were clouds on the horizon in the shape of some serious personnel worries. In defence, Rieper was ineligible – having signed after the UEFA deadline – while Boyd was out through suspension. In attack, Regi Blinker was still out after having his shoulder dislocated in a tackle with Rob Jones in the first leg. Liverpool on their part had been able to strengthen their side with the addition of star striker Robbie Fowler.

A lot would depend on Jansen's team selection. Curbing the attacking threat of Steve McManaman, along with the duo of Fowler and Owen, would be the key to the outcome. Not for the first time the Dutchman came up with a team selection which no one would have predicted. Jansen chose a back three of Mahé, Stubbs and Annoni to cope with Liverpool's attacking threat. David Hannah was drafted into a five-man midfield and – against all the odds – Tosh McKinlay found himself starting a game as a replacement for Blinker. McKinlay would have to play the same kind of attacking role which McNamara had done in the first game.

It was McKinlay who provided the moment which could have won the tie. At 2–2 Liverpool were through – by virtue of their two away goals counting double in the event of a tie. Playing in front of their own

Celtic's Bald Eagle: cult hero Rico Annoni

crowd, Liverpool were content to soak up pressure with only occasional forays into attack. Celtic needed a goal and, in 20 minutes, McKinlay came down the left and threw in a cross which caused panic in the Liverpool defence. The erratic David James came for the ball and got into a tangle with Bjornebye which allowed the ball to drop for Simon Donnelly. With James stranded, Donnelly elected to try a lob which sailed over, with the goal at his mercy. Afterwards Donnelly conceded that he had perhaps taken the ball a little early and had more time than he realised. Nonetheless, Celtic took encouragement from the near-miss and only minutes later felt robbed when Bjornebye headed a Wieghorst shot off the line. Not only were they unlucky in the clearance, the Celtic players were adamant that Bjornebye had also used a hand.

At the other end the Celtic defence was performing heroically. Enrico Annoni had become a fan's favourite at Celtic, but they had seen more of Lord Lucan so far this season than they had of their beloved 'Rico'. Apart from a few appearances on the subs bench, Annoni had not kicked a ball in anger. Against Liverpool, however, he was immense. Jansen said he had been impressed with the Italian in training and knew he could do the job. Annoni fully repaid Jansen's confidence with a Man-of-the-Match performance, which – along with Stubbs and Mahé – completely snuffed out Liverpool's attacking threat. Liverpool

Frenchman Stephane Mahe added bite to the Celtic defence

never really looked like scoring until a few minutes from the end when a Reidle shot beat Gould, but Donnelly was there to clear it off the line. The game ended goalless and Liverpool went through on the away-goals rule. Celtic left Anfield bloodied but unbowed and, just as they had in the Cup-Winners' Cup more than 30 years previously, ruing the mistakes of the first leg which had cost them the tie.

Any post-European hangover would have to be quickly dealt with. Celtic would have to get over the disappointment of another early European exit in time to take on Kilmarnock at Celtic Park. Kilmarnock had become, if not a bogey team, then certainly a thorn in Celtic's flesh in recent years. Although Killie had never won at Celtic Park, they had only lost two of their last six Premiership encounters against Celtic and another two of those games ended in draws – which had cost Celtic dearly in their bid to win the league over the past two seasons. Celtic, in the aftermath of the Liverpool game, were in no mood for any nonsense.

Almost from the first blast of the referee's whistle they were roared on by a capacity crowd, many of whom had made the midweek trip down to Liverpool and were intent on showing their appreciation for a side which was looking more impressive with every game. With a more familiar line-up featuring the return of Boyd and Rieper, Celtic started quietly but confidently, Craig Burley serving notice of his intentions just on the quarter-hour mark with a fierce shot which Lekovic was fortunate to deal with. This acted as a catalyst and the new Celtic midfield pairing of Burley and Wieghorst, aided and abetted by Thom and McNamara, simply ran the game from then on. They took the match by the scruff of the neck and shook it until it was dead which, as it turned out, only took about 20 minutes. In 17 minutes Celtic were in front when Thom threaded a ball through to Henrik Larsson who struck it sweetly past Lekovic from about 12 yards out. Celtic continued to press with everything coming through the midfield. Kilmarnock had no response and, at times, Lekovic was single-handedly having to deal with six Celtic attackers as the four midfielders poured forward behind Larsson and Donnelly. The game was settled within a five-minute period.

In 32 minutes, McNamara and Wieghorst linked up to carve open the Kilmarnock defence and send the ball through to Donnelly. Lekovic, who would perform heroics for Kilmarnock, managed to get a hand to the shot and, although he turned it onto the far post, it still rebounded into the net. Two minutes later it was Wieghorst's turn, when he played a delightful one-two with

Jansen's conversion of Morten Wieghorst into an attacking midfielder gave the Dane a new lease of life and revived his international career

Wieghorst gets in on the act with Celtic's third against Killie

Donnelly, then ran on and took a moment to steady himself before shooting past Lekovic. Then, in 37 minutes, Larsson got his own second and Celtic's fourth. Thom chipped the ball forward from a quickly taken free-kick – these would become a hallmark of Celtic's play – and Larsson was there with a neat header which beat the keeper.

Celtic went in at half-time four goals ahead and expecting more in the second half. Kilmarnock were in disarray and had no real answer. They seldom threatened – which can be seen by the match statistics which show that they had only three shots on target to Celtic's eighteen. There was no question of Celtic taking it easy in the second half, they continued to press and only Lekovic denied them a more convincing win. There can't be many goalkeepers who go away on the wrong end of a four-goal thumping able to take heart that they have played a great game.

The Kilmarnock game took Celtic's unbeaten run to ten, earning Wim Jansen the Bell's Manager of the Month award for September and giving Henrik Larsson the Player of the Month award. While they may

Larsson scores Celtic's opener against Kilmarnock

Larsson grabs the final goal in a 4–0 rout of Kilmarnock

A Parkhead double: Jansen is Bell's Manager of the Month and Larsson is Player of the Month.

have been out of Europe, there was a strong suspicion that domestic success was not far away.

Celtic 4   Kilmarnock 0
Donnelly
Larsson (2)
Wieghorst

Celtic: Gould, Boyd, Rieper, Stubbs, Mahé, McNamara, Burley, Wieghorst, Thom, Larsson, Donnelly

Substitutes: McKinlay for Thom, Annoni for Stubbs, Hannah for Wieghorst

Bookings: None

Attendance: 48,165

THE FIRST TEST

Hearts v Celtic
18 October 1997

Ibrox had proved to be a less-than-happy hunting ground for Celtic in recent years. Apart from their inability to beat Rangers, it had also been the scene of two of their most embarrassing results of recent years. In 1994 at Ibrox, Celtic lost to Raith Rovers on penalties in the final of the Coca-Cola Cup. More recently, it was only a matter of months since Celtic had been taken to two games before losing to Falkirk in the semi-final of the previous season's Scottish Cup. So, not surprisingly, there was some talk of an Ibrox hoodoo as Celtic prepared for the semi-final of the Coca-Cola Cup. When you consider that they were drawn against Dunfermline, who were the last side to beat them, then such talk was given a little more credence than it might otherwise have deserved.

Given the recent history between the two teams, Celtic, who had Blinker back for his first game after dislocating his shoulder against Liverpool, gave Dunfermline a lot of respect, possibly a bit more than they deserved. The Celtic play in the first half was patient without being totally in command. Dunfermline caused problems with high balls into the Celtic half which the Celtic defenders, uncharacteristically, did not deal with as tidily as the fans had become used to. In short, it was a below-par performance with a number of Celtic players not firing on all cylinders. Celtic were lucky not to go in a goal down when Bingham, who had scored against them at Celtic Park, outstripped the Celtic defence just before half-time, but then shot wide with only Gould to beat.

Wim Jansen's half-time team talk plainly did the trick and there was more of a cutting edge to Celtic's performance in the next 45 minutes. Jackie McNamara began to get further forward and with each excursion

This Burley effort was unsuccessful but he would get the only goal of the game in the Coca-Cola Cup semi-final against Dunfermline

into the Dunfermline half he found more and more space. However, with the Dunfermline defence sitting in for most of the game, shooting chances were few and far between, with the Celtic forwards having to content themselves with long-range efforts from outside the box. Some of the Celtic players with longer memories, including McNamara, began to feel that it might be Falkirk all over again. In 69 minutes, however, the deadlock was broken when Larsson gathered the ball just inside the 18-yard area. Spotting Burley to his right, the Swedish international slipped the ball to his midfielder and Burley fired a fierce shot past Westwater into the Dunfermline goal.

Once they had gone in front Celtic never looked like losing and began to play more and more of their own style of football. For Dunfermline it was a case of what might have been. With only seconds left in the game they came as close as they will ever get to forcing extra-time and with it, who knows what. The referee had already looked at his watch when the ball broke to Hamish French. With the dying seconds of

Tom Boyd won his fiftieth cap and captained Scotland as they beat Latvia at Celtic Park to qualify for the World Cup finals in France

the match ticking away he fired a low drive through a scrum of bodies. It looked like a goal from the moment it left his boot but Gould, who hadn't had a save to make all night, saw it late and managed to turn it past the post. Once again, as he had done against St Johnstone in the league, Gould had performed heroics when it mattered.

'It was the last minute of the semi-final,' recalls the goalkeeper, 'and Hamish hit one from outside the box and it came through a ruck of players. It was more of a satisfying save for a goalkeeper than the George O'Boyle one because you really need to have quick feet and get a good solid hand on the ball.'

Gould's last-minute effort ensured that Celtic had won the game and ended their so-called Ibrox hoodoo. Which was just as well because with Hampden still out of action, Celtic would be back at Ibrox in a few weeks for their first Cup final in two and a half years.

Celtic Park was full again on Saturday, 11 October but this time Scotland were the home team. Celtic Park played host to the final World Cup qualifying tie against Latvia. It was a big game for Scotland – their 2–0 win took them into the finals in France the following summer – and a number of Celtic players played their part. Tom Boyd captained the side in honour of reaching his fiftieth international cap, while Craig Burley, Tosh McKinlay and Simon Donnelly all took part, with Jackie McNamara on the subs bench.

Celtic's Scottish contingent, as well as others such as Larsson,

Wieghorst and Rieper who had also been on World Cup duty for their countries, had a week to recover from their international exertions. Their return to domestic duty saw them facing a game which, in the absence of the postponed first Old Firm fixture, would be the most serious test to date of their championship aspirations. Celtic had now climbed to third place in the table. They were one point behind Rangers and three points behind Hearts, although both the Old Firm clubs had a game in hand on the Edinburgh side. Hearts had emerged as the surprise leaders of the Premier League and were playing fast, attractive football with a combination of home-grown stars, including a clutch of emerging youngsters, and a sprinkling of Continental players. Under the astute managership of Jim Jefferies they considered themselves championship contenders and while the rest of Scottish football waited for the bubble to burst, Hearts just kept on winning.

Celtic knew that they would have to be at their most disciplined in the game against Hearts and that, indeed, was how they started the game. But there's no doubt that their cause was aided by some strange tactics from Jim Jefferies who elected, in a home game, to effectively play with only one striker, in the shape of Jim Hamilton. The Celtic defence was never really threatened in the early stages and once again it was Celtic who got the important early goal. In 15 minutes Regi Blinker took a corner on the left and the ball deflected to Henrik Larsson. Larsson turned it out to Marc Rieper, who was just inside the penalty box, and the Danish international controlled it on his chest, allowed it to drop and then volleyed an unstoppable shot past Gilles Rousset in the Hearts goal. Celtic were one up and looking good.

Over the years the Celtic support, and certain sectors of the management, have acquired a decent-sized chip on their shoulder about their treatment at the hands of referees. The legendary Jock Stein was fond of alleging that 'we get nothing' from the men in black. But even Stein would have applauded referee John Rowbotham for a superb decision which all but gave Celtic the points against Hearts. With 21 minutes gone, Burley was fouled by Salvatori inside the Hearts half. When Rowbotham didn't give the foul Burley was furious. But what Burley, and almost everyone else except the referee, hadn't spotted was Regi Blinker making a run on the left. The ball broke to Blinker and –

thanks to Mr Rowbotham allowing a superb advantage decision – he was able to fire in a cross which Larsson gratefully turned in at the back post. Celtic were 2–0 up, Hearts were incensed, but the decision was absolutely correct.

Celtic continued to press in the second half with Blinker hitting the bar and Larsson having a goal quite correctly disallowed for using his hand to control the ball. It was really all Celtic, and Hearts would not have had a look in but for the sort of defensive lapse which the Celtic fans hoped had been banished under Jansen. Hearts had brought on veteran striker John Robertson for Hamilton and he was beginning to cause problems for the Celtic defence, especially Stubbs. The defender was starting to feel the effects of two injuries he had picked up in the first half and Robertson was starting to turn him. It was Robertson who was able to send in a cross, which the Celtic defence could not clear and, after it took several bounces, Colin Cameron hit a shot which came off a defender and past Gould. This was Hearts' best spell of the match. A few minutes later, the heroic Stubbs headed off the line and Gould was able to smother Cameron's shot on the rebound. Celtic, too, had their chances but with two minutes to go it was Gould once again who made sure of the points with a fine save from a David Weir shot.

Celtic had met their toughest test and passed with flying colours. They had now completed the first quarter of the league programme, barring that postponed Rangers game, and found themselves second in the league only a point behind their oldest rivals.

Celtic 2	Hearts 1
Rieper	Cameron
Larsson	

Celtic: Gould, Boyd, Stubbs, Rieper, Mahé, McNamara, Burley, Wieghorst, Blinker, Donnelly, Larsson

Substitutes: Thom for Blinker, Hannah for Donnelly

Bookings: Burley, Boyd, Wieghorst, Larsson

Attendance: 16,997

TOP OF THE LEAGUE

St Johnstone v Celtic
25 October 1997

From the day it was founded in 1888, Celtic has always been a club which has remained proud of its charitable origins. Under chairman Fergus McCann there have been more tangible signs of those charitable beginnings with the homeless and the under-privileged frequently being guests of the club at Celtic Park. Similarly, the players are encouraged to become active in various club initiatives which is why, for example, a number of first-team stars found themselves ladling out hot soup at a soup kitchen in the centre of Glasgow.

Chairman Fergus McCann hands over a cheque to Liz Lockhard from the Loaves and Fishes appeal after Celtic players spent the evening manning a soup kitchen

There are times, of course, when charity can go too far. Certainly the Celtic supporters had felt that giving the other nine teams six points of a start in the Premier Division was perhaps a touch excessive. The players plainly felt the same way, because since those unfortunate games against Hibs and Dunfermline the dual values of thrift and hard work had taken over. Nowhere was that more obvious than in the Celtic defence which, since the signing of Marc Rieper, had taken on a much more settled look. As a consequence, by the time they faced St Johnstone in the league they had conceded only four goals in the eight domestic fixtures since the clubs had last met. Rieper and Stubbs were solid as a rock at the centre; Tom Boyd was redoubtable out on the right; and the fierce tackling of Stephane Mahé on the other side left no opposition forward in any doubt that they had been in a game. Behind these four was Jonathan Gould, the stop-gap goalkeeper who was now commanding a regular place as an automatic first choice. Gould's shot-stopping abilities, combined with the concentration to pull off important saves late in the game, made the Celtic defence a formidable unit.

It may have come as something of a surprise to the capacity crowd that the Celtic defence was put to a severe test in the early part of what, or so the fans assumed, should have been a straightforward game against St Johnstone. Had Celtic after all not stretched their unbeaten run to 12 games? Who were St Johnstone to try to make it unlucky 13?

Certainly as the game began there were signs that some of the Celtic players might have been thinking along those lines. There was a certain lack of urgency in the attacking play – as if being on the park was enough to bring the goals by divine right. It was the Celtic defenders who were doing most of the work in the first quarter of an hour. With less than ten minutes on the clock, Gould had to be at full stretch and even then only managed to tip a Jenkinson corner over the bar. A few minutes later Gould was the saviour again when he made a fine stop from a Sekerlioglu header. In the fourteenth minute the Celtic defence were uncharacteristically at sixes and sevens trying to deal with another Saints corner but, with the defenders in disarray and the ball breaking to Dasovic, the St Johnstone defender could only shoot past the post.

Just when Saints were beginning to think they might be able to create an upset, the Celtic strikers stirred themselves out of their lethargy. Shots began to rain in on Alan Main in the St Johnstone goal. The Perth keeper had international aspirations and he certainly got the chance to display his form in this game. First, Blinker fired a screaming shot just over the bar, followed by another which Main took two attempts to hold. Moments later with Main beaten by a Wieghorst header, up popped John O'Neil to stick out his knee on the goal line and prevent a certain goal. Celtic were queuing up to shoot. McNamara hit a post, Donnelly had a header saved on the line and even Alan Stubbs came foraging forward only to be denied when his shot was saved by Main in inspired form.

The goal had to come and not even Alan Main in this kind of form could keep a rampant Celtic

Regi Blinker bemoans another missed chance – a sight which would become all too familiar as his season turned into a personal nightmare

attack out for much longer. That was indeed the case, but Main could curse his luck for finally being beaten. In 31 minutes a relatively harmless ball came into the Saints half and Dasovic attempted to head the ball safely back to Main. What he hadn't seen was that Henrik Larsson had continued his run and when Dasovic's header fell well short of the keeper, the Swede was able to dart in and score to put Celtic ahead. Three minutes later Celtic were 2–0 up after a move which saw their midfield cut through St Johnstone like a knife through butter. McNamara started things out on the right by cutting the ball inside to Donnelly, who then played a one-two with Blinker before sending the ball crisply to Morten

Wieghorst. The Danish international spotted Mahé making a run down the left and rolled the ball neatly into his path but, before the Frenchman could continue his run, he was pulled down by McQuillan. The referee had no hesitation in awarding a penalty, which Donnelly converted as he had been doing all season. Thirty-four minutes gone, Celtic were two ahead, and the game was finished as a contest.

The second half was pretty much a procession as Celtic controlled the game from start to finish. St Johnstone had a final flurry in the eightieth minute when George O'Boyle, who had come on as a substitute, unleashed a fierce drive. If it had gone in who knows what might have happened but, just as he had done earlier in the season, Gould again denied O'Boyle with a superb one-handed save. By this time, however, Celtic fans had all but lost interest in a game that had been well won for almost an hour. They were much more absorbed with a radio commentary from Tannadice where Rangers were drawing 1–1 with Dundee United. The terracing mathematicians had worked out that if the results stayed the same then Celtic would be joint top of the league on points at least. The roar which announced a United penalty was deafening, the roar which greeted them scoring with that penalty almost took the newly acquired roof off the stadium. Rangers had lost 2–1 and Celtic were top of the league. So much for unlucky 13.

No one could have foreseen after that dismal start that, within seven games, Celtic would overcome their two-game handicap and head the division. The trick would be to stay there.

Celtic 2   St Johnstone 0
Larsson
Donnelly

Celtic: Gould, Boyd, Rieper, Stubbs, Mahé, McNamara, Burley, Wieghorst, Blinker, Larsson, Donnelly

Substitutes: O'Donnell for Blinker, Hannah for Larsson

Bookings: None

Attendance: 48,545

SLEEVES ROLLED UP

Dunfermline v Celtic
1 November 1997

Hard as it may have been to predict two weeks into the season, being top of the league at the end of the first quarter was not entirely new to the Celtic faithful. It had happened before in previous seasons, but it had never lasted and, come May, they had finished second behind Rangers. Being top of the league in November after eight games was one thing, but being top after 36 games was what mattered most. Celtic's claim to be genuine contenders would be given its sternest test during the month of November. In the space of the month they would have to face Rangers twice – at home and away – take on Dundee United in the league, and there was also the small matter of the Coca-Cola Cup final – also against Dundee United – later in the month. But, before all that, there was still a tough league game against Dunfermline to be dealt with.

The Pars had proved a handful already for Celtic. Apart from losing 2–1 at home in the second league match of the season, Celtic had not found it easy to beat them by the narrowest of margins in the Coca-Cola Cup final. Taking them on at East End Park was not going to be anyone at Celtic's idea of a day at the beach. One of the factors which had contributed to Celtic's lengthy unbeaten run was a team spirit which had built itself up by virtue of being able to field a virtually unchanged side. Barring injury or suspension, the Celtic side pretty much picked itself these days. This settled side had begun to display an uncanny understanding of the way each other played. The back four could be relied on to move the ball quickly into the midfield, which then had the option of the surging forward runs of Burley and Wieghorst or the wide running of Blinker and the born-again midfielder McNamara. They could then fire in probing diagonal balls for Larsson or Donnelly to

After a shaky start, Wim Jansen and his second-in-command, Murdo MacLeod, had Celtic firing on all cylinders

connect with. If the two strikers chose to hold up the ball instead, then they were sure of four midfielders streaming forward in support as supplementary attackers. It was a team which Wim Jansen had fashioned to be capable of switching from defence to attack – and vice versa – in the time it took for a single pass. It was also a team which was not yet finished. Jansen had been pursuing players for some time and there would be another new face within a matter of days with the promise of more to come.

The game against Dunfermline was the first test of Celtic's mental toughness. Dunfermline, having beaten Celtic once and come close on a second occasion, committed themselves to an uncharacteristically bold attacking formation. Manager Bert Paton fielded a team which contained three forwards in the shape of George Shaw, Andy Smith and Gerry Britton. As a former Celt, albeit a fringe member of the squad, Britton had good reason to do well against his old club. Dunfermline started the game with the air of men with something to prove, if only to themselves. Their pace and aggression unsettled Celtic who were unable to break forward themselves. Whenever possible Dunfermline denied the Celtic players space, tackling feverishly and shutting down all the passing options as soon as they presented themselves. Celtic, for their part, never really got going in the first half and seldom threatened Ian Westwater in the Dunfermline goal.

Obviously Wim Jansen's half-time talk emphasised that this was not going to be a game won by a display of silky footballing skills. This was turning into an old-fashioned blood and snotters Scottish Premiership game and the team which would win would be the team that was prepared to collectively roll its sleeves up and get on with the job in hand. Celtic started the second half in a much more positive mood and as they fed the ball more and more to McNamara out on the right, the former Dunfermline player found himself getting more and more change out of his old club's defence. Despite Celtic being on top almost from the moment that the whistle blew for the start of the second half, there were still no goals. It was beginning to look like the sort of game which would only be won by a flash of inspiration or a stroke of luck.

Celtic supporters have often claimed that theirs is not a lucky team. However, few could deny that in the 1997–98 season they carried their luck on more than one occasion. There are those who would also argue that a team makes its own luck, and chief among them on this occasion would be Regi Blinker. The Dutchman had been welcomed with open arms at Celtic Park and embraced by fans who had become used to seeing quality wingers. However, he had yet to fully realise his potential and there were those who were beginning to feel that he was flattering to deceive. The Dunfermline game was another where, once again, Blinker did all the fancy footwork but failed to deliver the telling final ball. In 67 minutes Blinker once again came down the left towards the Dunfermline penalty area. With Greg Shields backing off and unwilling to make the challenge, Blinker attempted a speculative shot from the edge of the area. Immediately he struck the ball it clipped Shields' outstretched foot and ballooned in a parabola which took it up and over the despairing Ian Westwater. A goal out of nothing put Celtic 1–0 ahead.

Dunfermline felt with some justification more than a little aggrieved to be behind and there was no question of their heads going down. They

*Marc Rieper led Celtic's aerial attacks against the Pars in the
Coca-Cola Cup*

continued to press for an equaliser but, by now, Jansen had Celtic well
schooled in the art of defending a single-goal lead. The defence sat in
and absorbed the pressure and relied on hitting Dunfermline on the
break. Even so, things were getting a little tense as Dunfermline threw
caution to the wind and poured forward in the hope of at least getting
a share of the points.

It was one of these last-ditch efforts by the home side which proved
to be their undoing. With only four minutes remaining on the clock, the
ball was slung forward to Colin Miller. But, almost before he had time
to gather the ball, McNamara pounced to dispossess him. McNamara
and Boyd then combined to work the ball up the field and into the path
of Henrik Larsson. Thanks to a perfectly weighted pass, Larsson was

off like a hare, dreadlocks flying behind him in his slipstream, as he outstripped the home defence as though they weren't there. With only Westwater to beat, Larsson appeared to have all the time in the world. The Swede feinted to shoot at the near post and as Westwater went in one direction, Larsson calmly fired the ball into the space left by the diving keeper.

Celtic had won 2–0. That made it 14 games unbeaten, eight wins in a row, and still top of the league. But to the fans none of this would matter because their next game would be the severest test of them all – Rangers at Ibrox.

Celtic 2   Dunfermline 0
Blinker
Larsson

Celtic: Gould, Boyd, Rieper, Stubbs, Mahé, McNamara, Burley, Wieghorst, Blinker, Larsson, Donnelly

Substitutes: Thom for Larsson

Bookings: Burley, Wieghorst, Blinker

Attendance: 12,627

OLD FIRM, NEW FACE

Rangers v Celtic
8 November 1997

Despite their undoubted skill and their newly found team spirit, Celtic did enjoy a share of good fortune in 1997–98 which had been denied them in previous seasons. One of those strokes of good fortune had been the postponement of their first league meeting with Rangers. If the two sides had met at Celtic Park as scheduled on 1 September, with Celtic only having the three points from three games and a team which was in transition and had still failed to gel, there is no telling what damage might have been done. As it was that game was now to be played on 19 November and Celtic would actually play their second Old Firm match of the season first. Nonetheless, even with a new sense of purpose and self-belief in the squad, it would be a vital 11 days for the club.

The build-up to an Old Firm game is invariably fraught with tension. On the debit side, there was backroom turmoil at Celtic Park with the departure of David Hay as assistant general manager. The tension also appeared to be getting to the players when Tosh McKinlay and Henrik Larsson had a training-ground spat which left Larsson with a badly bruised nose and eyes. Larsson's injuries were not serious enough to cause him to miss a game. McKinlay, who had appeared to be out of favour with Jansen up till that point, effectively went into internal exile. Although Craig Brown kept him in the Scotland squad and, ultimately, took him to France where he played in the World Cup finals, McKinlay made only two more appearances for Celtic under Jansen, both of them as substitute.

On the credit side, Celtic had a new player. Jansen had been pursuing Paul Lambert of Borussia Dortmund since he saw him play for Scotland against Belarus in September. General manager Jock Brown had been tracking the player, but Dortmund were reluctant to part with a player they had come to value so highly. However, it was no secret that Lambert's wife had not settled in Germany and was keen to return to Scotland. The German club bowed to the inevitable and gave Celtic permission to talk to the player and personal terms were quickly settled. It was then a question of when he would be released. Initially Dortmund wanted to hang on until their Champions

A welcome sight: Paul Lambert joins Celtic from Borussia Dortmund

League commitments were completed in mid-December. However, manager Nevio Scala decided he could be released sooner. Lambert made an emotional farewell to the Dortmund fans on Wednesday, 5 November, and signed for Celtic the following day for a fee of just under £2 million. Lambert's arrival caused intense speculation among the fans and the media. He was eligible to play against Rangers 48 hours later but would Jansen take the gamble? The smart media money was on Lambert being used to snuff out the threat of Paul Gascoigne in a man-marking job at Ibrox. The speculation was academic because Jansen and Lambert had already discussed the matter when the midfielder signed and both men had agreed that he would not start the game. Larsson, however, would. After the training-ground incident he had flown to Sweden for his father-in-law's funeral but he was back in time and would start the game.

The rivalry between Celtic and Rangers is intense, but now there was an air of desperation creeping into the minds of the Celtic fans. The previous season Celtic had lost all four league games against their main rivals. In fact, it had been nine games, stretching over 30 months, since Celtic had beaten Rangers in the league. While the Rangers fans had been taunting their Celtic counterparts with chants about winning ten league titles in a row, the Rangers players knew that they could make it ten derby games without a win for Celtic. Despite eight wins in a row in the league up till now, you would be hard-pressed to find a media

Anxious moments: Stubbs is injured in a clash with Marco Negri in the first Old Firm game of the season

pundit on match day who was willing to tip Celtic to extend that run at Ibrox.

In the past Celtic had often been the architects of their own downfall against Rangers, as cavalier attacking, combined with naïve defending and foolish mistakes, allowed the Ibrox side to score on the counter. This time there was a solidity about the Celtic defence which suggested they would not be caught quite so easily. Even so, Jonathan Gould was in action within a few minutes to fend off a rasping drive from Paul Gascoigne. Celtic, though, were prepared to sit in and allow Rangers to come at them, allowing the central combination of Stubbs and Rieper to break up attacks with Boyd and Mahé taking care of the flanks. The game plan started to go wrong in just 16 minutes. Stubbs jumped for the ball with Marco Negri and the Italian's flailing elbow accidentally caught the Celtic defender in the eye. Stubbs had to be stretchered off with an injury which fortunately turned out not to be as severe as it looked. Nonetheless, he sat out the rest of the game and Enrico Annoni

Marc Rieper and Richard Gough engage in aerial combat

came on to take his place. Annoni played well, as he had against Liverpool, but it took time for the defence to settle again.

In between times Larsson, on one of Celtic's rare excursions into the Rangers half, had two marvellous shots splendidly saved by Goram. The Rangers keeper was having his usual maddeningly impeccable game against Celtic. Tommy Burns suggested that when he died it might be written on his gravestone that: 'Andy Goram broke my heart.' The game was less than half-an-hour old and already Jansen and Larsson might have chipped in for similar inscriptions of their own. Three minutes later the game was turned Rangers' way when Laudrup got the better of Stephane Mahé and sent over a low cross to defender Richard Gough, of all people, who was lurking in the Celtic penalty box and he instinctively turned the ball into the net. Rangers were a goal ahead, and with Laudrup and Gascoigne dominating the middle of the park Celtic never really looked like catching them.

In the second half Celtic continued to attack, but the game was slipping away from them. Jansen's team selection had ceded midfield superiority to the opposition. Celtic were playing with a four-man midfield, Rangers were playing with five in the middle and making the extra man count. The five-man midfield meant that no matter how resolutely Celtic defended, and Rieper in particular was excellent, they had great difficulty in being able to link up with the forwards and mount any kind of counter-attack. The midfield and the forwards played without passion and allowed Rangers to boss the game.

Jansen tried to change things around by committing another two substitutes. He sent on Andreas Thom for Blinker on the hour mark, then Lambert made his first appearance in a Celtic shirt when he replaced Tom Boyd with quarter of an hour to go. The new faces could not improve the situation and although Gould had nothing to do in the second half the game was beyond his team-mates. The final indignity for Celtic came nine minutes from time when Mahé was sent off for his second bookable offence. Ten-man Celtic managed to hold out until the end and, even though half the team were making their Old Firm debuts, they trooped off to the familiar jeers and victory chants from the Rangers fans which Celtic players had had to endure for 30 months.

The game against Rangers was a major setback for the new Celtic. They had been ineffectual and, by and large, had failed to compete. They were no longer top of the league and, thanks to Hearts beating Hibs in the Edinburgh derby, they had now slipped to third. Not only that, they would have to play Rangers again in just over a week.

Celtic 0   Rangers 1
                       Gough

Celtic: Gould, Boyd, Rieper, Stubbs, Mahé, McNamara, Burley, Wieghorst, Blinker, Donnelly, Larsson

Substitutes: Annoni for Stubbs, Thom for Blinker, Lambert for Boyd

Bookings: Boyd, Burley, Blinker

Sendings off: Mahé

Attendance: 50,082

ONE OF THOSE DAYS

Motherwell v Celtic
15 November 1997

Paul Lambert's Celtic debut may not have been his most memorable game, but he was in no doubt that he had made the right move in giving up the Bundesliga for the Premier Division. His 18 months in Germany had been the making of the player after he became one of the first Scots to move to Europe under the freedom of contract provided by the Bosman judgement. Lambert had become a favourite at St Mirren – where he won a Scottish Cup medal at the age of 17 – before moving to Motherwell. But, in the summer of 1996, he became a free agent and although a number of clubs in Scotland and England made vague approaches it was Borussia Dortmund who came up with the three-year deal. Lambert was bought as a squad player but quickly forced his way into the side and capped a fairy tale first season by playing in every Champions League match – including the final which Dortmund won 3–1 against Juventus.

Lambert had become a favourite with the Dortmund fans who respected and understood his decision to return home. On his final game in Germany, against Parma, many of the Dortmund fans wore Celtic strips and chanted 'Celtic' as he took his leave of them. For Lambert it was a more intense experience than the European Cup final but he had no reservations about the move.

'I have left a big club to come to one of equal stature,' he said at the time of the move. 'No way have I taken a step down. I won the highest honour in the club game with Dortmund and I would love to do it here. I've made the right decision and I'll be giving it my best shot. I've played in the Champions League for the past two seasons and I see no reason why I shouldn't be competing in it next year again. I know what it's like to win things and I believe I can add to my medal haul with Celtic this season.'

Lambert was the eighth new player to join Celtic this season and his own ambitions matched those of the club. These players were all bought with the express purpose of shaping a team to win the Scottish Premier Division and, as such, compete at the highest level of European club football. The arrival of Lambert was another piece in Wim Jansen's jigsaw. He had never been a prolific goalscorer, but his time in Germany had honed his skills as a defensive midfielder. Jansen saw Lambert as someone who could hold the line in the middle of the park allowing Burley to go forward to join the attack. He could successfully break down opposition attacks and then, with his devastatingly accurate distribution, which at times evoked comparison with the great Paul McStay, Lambert also provided Celtic with more options in turning defence into attack.

His first full game for Celtic was, ironically, against Motherwell – the club he had left to go to Germany. Lambert took his place alongside Craig Burley in the engine-room of the Celtic midfield, with Wieghorst left on the bench. There were other enforced changes in the Celtic line up because of the suspension of Stephane Mahé after his sending off against Rangers. Jansen was asked, given that he had lost one left-back, would this mean a place for Scotland's left-back Tosh McKinlay? His answer was an emphatic no and it was David Hannah who filled in for Mahé. One piece of good news for Celtic was that Alan Stubbs' eye injury had not proved serious. There were fears that he might have fractured a cheek-bone but it turned out to be simply bruising which had eased sufficiently in the week to allow to him to take his place against Motherwell.

It was Elvis Presley who asked in *GI Blues* if you had ever had one of those days? The sort where, as the great man put it, 'nothing goes right from morning till night'. After this match against Motherwell, Celtic would be able to answer with an emphatic yes. On the face of it, this game was the ideal opportunity to get back on the rails after losing to Rangers. Motherwell were bottom of the league, a position they would flirt with for most of the season. They also had major injury problems with five first-team regulars and they had only 14 fit men available for the game at Celtic Park. Celtic certainly started the game as if someone was going to pay for the Rangers defeat. Woods in the

Motherwell goal had to be at his peak to deny the Celtic attacks which rained in for the first 20 minutes. Stubbs, surging forward to join the attack, had one shot brilliantly saved and another header cleared off the line. Larsson headed off the crossbar, there was another clearance off the line and then Woods had to pull off another spectacular save from McNamara.

It was one-way traffic and, in the middle of it, Celtic even managed to get the ball into the net. However, referee Willie Young who was having, to be kind, an over-zealous sort of an afternoon ruled Larsson offside after he had headed home from a Burley cross. Burley himself would also have a goal chalked off later in the half. Young's constant use of the whistle made the game a stop-start affair which really prevented Celtic building any kind of rhythm. Even so, the fans believed it was only a matter of time before the goal came. Unfortunately it was at the wrong end. Motherwell won a free-kick in the middle of the park and Ross sent it into the penalty box. Owen Coyle was first to it and, although he was shaping to shoot, Gould appeared to have it covered. Coyle's shot, however, took a deflection off McCulloch and trickled past the helpless Gould and into the net. Unbelievably, given the balance of play, Celtic were a goal down.

Things got worse before half-time. In 36 minutes Regi Blinker got into a tussle with Motherwell's Kevin Christie. The Celtic winger was adjudged to have used an elbow and the referee had no hesitation in reaching for the red card and Blinker was on his way to the tunnel. Celtic had been badly hampered the previous season by an appalling disciplinary record which had lost them key players through suspension at crucial times. Jansen appeared to have knocked that unfortunate habit on the head, but now he had had two players red-carded in successive games.

Even with ten men, Celtic continued their assault on the Motherwell goal in the second half. Again Woods was inspired and his defence had all the luck that was going. As the attacks came to nothing, Celtic began to lose their shape – and their discipline – as they chased an equaliser. Jansen spent the game alternately staring down at his shoes – a trademark gesture when things were not going well – or screaming instructions from the dugout. As Celtic pushed forward, inevitably, they left gaps at the back, especially with only ten men. Fifteen minutes from time, Coyle slipped through the defence but shot wide. But, right on the stroke of full time, it was Coyle again who did damage when he evaded a tackle from Stubbs and easily rounded Annoni. He was left with only the keeper to beat but, as Gould came out, Coyle slipped the ball across to Mickey Weir who had all the time in the world to score.

Unbelievably, Celtic had lost 2–0. Rangers had only managed a draw at Aberdeen, but that was small consolation. They were back where they were at the start of the season. They had lost two in a row, they were only one game away from a crisis and their next match was against Rangers.

Celtic 0	Motherwell 2
	Coyle
	Weir

Celtic: Gould, Hannah, Rieper, Stubbs, Boyd, McNamara, Burley, Lambert, Blinker, Larsson, Donnelly

Substitutes: Wieghorst for Hannah, Thom for Donnelly, Annoni for Lambert

Bookings: Rieper, Wieghorst

Sendings off: Blinker

Attendance: 48,010

BACK FROM THE BRINK

Rangers v Celtic
19 November 1997

Celtic had begun the month of November with cautious optimism. They were top of the league, they were in the Coca-Cola Cup final and they had just added a top-class midfielder to the squad. Within a fortnight it had all gone horribly wrong, with two defeats, two players sent off and not a goal to their credit. This perceived lack of fire-power would become a recurring criticism as Celtic made many more chances than they took.

Under the circumstances, it is difficult to overestimate the importance of this re-arranged midweek fixture against Rangers. Another defeat would have been nothing short of catastrophic and all of the good work which had been done to recover from the start of the season would have simply been for nothing. Jansen had learned his lesson from the first game, in which his players had been swamped in the midfield when he played 4-4-2 against Rangers' 3-5-2 formation. This time Jansen would also pick a 3-5-2 line-up. With Blinker unavailable because of his red card against Motherwell, the team more or less picked itself. Wieghorst, who had had to make way for Lambert against Motherwell, was now able to play alongside him and Burley in the middle of the park. McNamara took his customary wing-back role on the right-hand side of the midfield, with Boyd moving up from defence to play on the left-hand side. Mahé, Rieper and Stubbs were the three at the back, with Larsson and Donnelly charged with breaking Celtic's striking duck up front.

Certainly Celtic were much more competitive in this match than they had been in the first game. There was no cushion of an eight-game winning streak, this time they were trying to avoid three defeats. For once, breaking Rangers' superiority in this fixture took on less

Morten Wieghorst launches a single-handed attack on the Rangers'
defence

importance than simply getting something from the game. Within the
first minute Celtic showed their mettle when Lambert cracked in a shot
from a Wieghorst pass which seemed headed for goal until it deflected
off a defender and went past for a corner. The corner was cleared, but
McNamara picked up the loose ball and himself went close. Celtic
were in the ascendancy and Rangers were once again prepared to sit

back and soak up pressure as they had done so often in these games. The pressure, however, was beginning to tell and the yellow cards began to pile up. Rangers captain Richard Gough was first in John Rowbotham's book for a foul on Larsson which almost ended in a goal for Celtic from the resulting free-kick. Rangers seldom threatened and it was more than half an hour before Gould was required to do anything. When Negri's header came from an Albertz free-kick Gould was more than capable of tipping it over the bar.

It was becoming a typical Old Firm game. Celtic continued to attack, Rangers defended resolutely, if a little nervously at first, and there were no goals. The only thing that mounted up in the first half were the yellow cards. In that first 45 minutes, referee Rowbotham dished out no fewer than eight bookings – three to Celtic, five to Rangers – as the pressure began to tell on everyone.

The second half started in much the same way as the first, with Rangers resolutely resisting Celtic pressure. Much of that pressure was coming down the Celtic left wing with Boyd and Wieghorst continually getting the better of the young Italian Rino Gattuso. But still it was the Rangers defence and Andy Goram who were able to deny Celtic any advantage. Whether or not the eight yellow cards had any effect on the players' performance in the second half is open to question, but the football did not seem as intense as in the first 45 minutes. It was still a pretty towsy affair and it came as no surprise when referee Rowbotham finally reached for the red card. In 59 minutes Paul Gascoigne and Morten Wieghorst went for the same ball just inside the Celtic half; there was a tussle and, while Wieghorst appeared to be holding Gascoigne back, the Rangers player lifted a hand and the Dane went down. John Rowbotham had no option but to send the Rangers player off and was greeted with a barrage of boos and jeers from the visiting fans for his trouble. Whether the contact made by Gascoigne was as serious as Wieghorst made out is debatable, but there is no doubt that Gascoigne did lift his hand which constitutes violent conduct. The England midfielder, who had led a charmed life with Scottish referees, found that his luck was running out.

Rangers were now down to ten men but, as Celtic quickly found out, the extra man didn't count for much. Rangers simply defended deeper and confined their attacks to sporadic breakaways. It was from one such breakaway in 69 minutes that Durie and Negri combined to set up a rare Rangers attack. Negri managed to get past Rieper but Stubbs was able to get in enough of a tackle to force the Italian to shoot wide. In 72 minutes Durie and Negri combined again and this time Stubbs could not reach him. The big Italian managed to get clear of Stubbs' tackle and as Gould tried to narrow the angle, he fired it past him at the near post to give Rangers a 1–0 lead.

Gould had been virtually faultless in the Celtic goal since he had taken over the gloves at the start of the season and it was a matter of genuine annoyance to him that he had been beaten at the near post, the position every goalkeeper should cover in this situation. Initially he felt he had allowed Negri too much room for the shot.

'I hate getting beaten at the near post and I don't think any goalkeeper is different,' Gould recalls. 'Actually, I think it was the pace of the ball that beat me. When I see it on telly now I realise it was a fair strike, I think you might have expected him to hit the ball across you, but he didn't. I think you have to be hard on yourself as a keeper. If you're not, then you take things a little too lightly. You set yourself standards and you dislike seeing any ball in the back of the net whether it be in training or in games. But as you become more experienced, you learn that if the ball goes in the back of the net at training it doesn't matter so much and the real time to get worried is on the pitch on a Saturday or Wednesday or whenever.'

Negri's goal was a carbon copy of so many which had been scored by Rangers against Celtic in the past. Rangers had contributed next to nothing to the game but had taken a half chance and were now in front. Celtic continued to press with Larsson, McNamara and Wieghorst all going close, with Goram once again pulling off a number of fine saves. Time was running out and, with the roar of the home crowd urging them on, Celtic surged forward, but it seemed to be in vain. But as the 90 minutes came and went with everyone looking at their watch and the Rangers fans urging the referee to blow for time-up, Celtic scored a miraculous injury-time goal. Celtic won a corner from the right – which didn't come to much – but Rangers did not clear quickly enough and the ball broke to McNamara on the right. He floated in a deep cross to the far post and Stubbs rose from a tangle of players to outjump Gough and head into the far corner of the net.

'It was quite similar to a lot of games against Rangers,' says Stubbs of the game. 'We were playing well, they attacked us in the second half, they hit us with a counter-attack and they scored from it. We were playing well and we had a number of chances and it just looked like it was going to be one of those nights when nothing was going to go for us. In the end I said to Marc with five or ten minutes to go: "I'm going up front. We need to get a goal, we've got nothing to lose." And he said: "Fine". I just looked over to the bench and told them and they had no

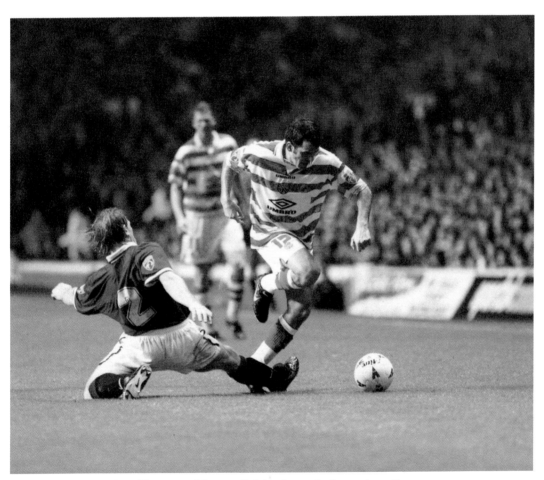

Darren Jackson hurdles a tackle as Celtic draw 1–1 against Rangers at Celtic Park

problems with that. It was just a cross in from Jackie, desperation stakes really, just get the ball into a dangerous area and hope we can get something from it.

'Jackie put a great ball in and because I was up front I just rose at the back post and as soon as I hit it I knew there was only one place it was going. It all happened very quickly for me as soon as I headed it. Goram was standing still, he knew it was in himself.'

The Celtic players were delirious. Darren Jackson, who had recovered from his illness and was now playing in his Old Firm debut, ran into the net to grab the ball and race back to the centre circle with it. Rangers were completely demoralised and it seemed like only seconds until the referee blew for full time. The Celtic fans behaved as though they had won the league and so did the players.

'It was like a victory for us,' recalls Alan Stubbs. 'It was injury time, the referee was going to blow up any minute and we went into the dressing-room as if we had taken three points off them. It came at the right time to give us the boost that we needed to go on again after two bad results. We had had a good run and then a couple of indifferent results, so it was important that we took something out of the Rangers game and it proved to be decisive in the end.'

Celtic 1   Rangers 1
Stubbs   Negri

Celtic: Gould, Rieper, Stubbs, Mahé, McNamara, Burley, Lambert,
    Wieghorst, Boyd, Larsson, Donnelly

Substitutes: Jackson for Donnelly, Thom for Boyd

Bookings: Mahé, Boyd, Wieghorst

Attendance: 49,509

AN IDEAL APPETISER

Dundee United v Celtic
22 November 1997

The last-gasp draw against Rangers had given the Celtic dressing-room a much needed boost, but there was still no disguising that two defeats and a draw was a pretty indifferent run of results. There was no respite from the pressure games either, because once again Celtic were involved in a Coca-Cola Cup double header. They would face Dundee United in the final at Ibrox on 30 November, but eight days before that they would have to take them on in the league at Celtic Park.

When the Celtic side lined up for that game, the fans could see just how much the draw against Rangers had cost them. Both centre-halves – Stubbs and Rieper – were injured and Burley was missing through suspension. On the other hand, Regi Blinker was now available again after serving his suspension and Andreas Thom was brought back. There was even a place on the bench for Tosh McKinlay. Celtic started the match with a back three of Boyd – showing his versatility by playing as a sweeper – David Hannah and Rico Annoni, who was starting his first league game in eight months. The four-man midfield had Lambert and Wieghorst in the centre in Burley's absence, with Stephane Mahé on the left and McNamara on the right. Thom was drafted in to join Larsson and Blinker in attack, with Jackson and Donnelly on the bench.

Thom had become an influential figure in his time at Celtic Park but his appearances could often be frustratingly brief. The German appeared to be injury prone and the Celtic fans had become used to the sight of him disappearing onto the bench after an hour or so. Jansen had used him mostly as a substitute and this match against Dundee United was Thom's first start since the 4–0 win against Kilmarnock on 4 October. As it turned out, whether by luck or judgement, Jansen's decision was inspired and Thom would play a key role in another emphatic win.

From the way the game started no one would have anticipated a comfortable Celtic victory. Dundee United had been turned over fairly comfortably in the game at Tannadice, but this was a different ball game. United had put together a decent run of results themselves, including that place in the Coca-Cola Cup final, and were determined to make more of a game of it this time. For the first half hour that seemed to consist of getting as many tangerine shirts behind the ball as possible and leaving Celtic to break them down. Celtic attacked patiently but, despite a somewhat erratic performance by Sieb Dykstra in goal for United, the goals did not appear to be coming. The fans were becoming impatient, they had seen this before against Motherwell and no one wanted a repeat of that result. United, meanwhile, were growing in confidence and mounted a few attacks of their own, and on one occasion only Gould's outstretched legs managed to stop Perry putting United in front.

The game turned in the thirty-first minute when Thom played a decisive part. McNamara got the ball inside the United half and sent the German on his way with another of his darting, diagonal runs. Thom looked up and saw Hannah in a great position by the back post but as he released the ball, Hannah was barged to the ground by Erik Pedersen. Thom stepped up and calmly slotted the penalty past Dykstra for his sixth goal of the season.

The opening goal settled Celtic and although it was only 1–0 at half-time, the game looked well within their reach. Celtic again started brightly in the second half with Thom's precision passing and accurate free-kicks setting up a number of chances. But United were not entirely out of the game. In 53 minutes Kjell Olofsson, who had scored against Celtic at Tannadice, fired over the bar after an error by Annoni. Moments later, Dundee United had the chance to change the entire complexion of the game when Winters beat both Boyd and Annoni in the Celtic box. His shot had Gould well beaten but it smacked harmlessly off the bottom of the post. United seemed to sense the moment was passing them by and, in 64 minutes, Henrik Larsson confirmed their suspicions. A neat passing move by Thom and

Donnelly set McNamara up in space. The young midfielder fired in a speculative shot which Dykstra managed to hold but then unaccountably spilled at the feet of Henrik Larsson. The Swede required no invitation to gather the ball and chip it over the prone Dykstra.

Celtic were now 2–0 up and coasting. Thom – who had been their key man – became more and more influential. Three minutes after Larsson scored, the Swede released Thom on the right but his vicious shot went past by less than a foot. In the seventy-first minute Thom got another chance in a similar move. This time the ball came from Wieghorst and this time his shot ended up in the corner of the net. Celtic could have finished the game there and then and simply played out the remaining 20 minutes, but with a Cup final coming up against the same opposition, it was important to do as much psychological damage as possible. In the seventy-ninth minute Larsson sealed what was an impressive Celtic display with a fourth goal. The Swedish striker had all the time in the world when he received a pass from Donnelly a few yards outside the area. He looked up and saw Dykstra off his line before audaciously chipping the keeper and sending the ball flying into the net.

United had arrived at Celtic Park full of hope and ambition and instead had been crushed and completely demoralised. They left knowing that they would have to come back down the motorway the following weekend to do it all again. This time against a full-strength Celtic side. For Celtic, however, the chance of winning their first silverware in two and a half years was now very much a reality.

Celtic 4   Dundee United 0
Thom (2)
Larsson (2)

Celtic: Gould, Annoni, Boyd, Hannah, McNamara, Wieghorst, Lambert,
     Mahé, Thom, Larsson, Blinker

Bookings: Hannah

Attendance: 48,010

France and Italy join forces to celebrate a Celtic triumph as Annoni and Mahe parade the Cup

THE MAIN COURSE

Coca-Cola Cup final

Dundee United v Celtic
30 November 1997

Even in its latest livery of Coca-Cola's red and white, the Scottish League Cup has never been a particularly happy tournament for Celtic. There have been glorious moments such as the famous 7–1 victory over Rangers, still a record score in a major British final, in 1957–58. On the other hand, there have been many more bad memories than good. Their last appearance in the final in 1994 was one of the most abject occasions in the club's recent history, when they lost on penalties to lowly Raith Rovers having been unable to beat them in 120 minutes of football. That defeat ranks beside Celtic's other famous hammering in the League Cup which came in 1971 when they were murdered 4–1 by Partick Thistle.

Celtic had appeared in 21 League Cup finals up till this one and had won only nine of them. To put that in even bleaker perspective, they had won only two of their last 13 League Cup final appearances. The last one had been 15 years ago in a tussle with Rangers which Celtic won 2–1. The scorer of the winning goal that day was Murdo MacLeod, now Celtic's assistant head coach. But it was MacLeod who pointed out before the game that this was a new Celtic side and there were no hoodoos, this team carried no baggage from the past. Whatever they did they would do for themselves and their future. There was no question of a League Cup jinx and the semi-final victory over Dunfermline had surely put paid to any talk of an Ibrox hoodoo.

As they prepared for the first final of the season, Wim Jansen was able to reflect on the fact that his injury worries were clearing up nicely and he had almost a full-strength squad to choose from. The most important news was that the centre-back pairing of Rieper and Stubbs would be fit and able to play. Rieper had missed the league match against Dundee United with a calf strain but was mending nicely. Likewise, Alan Stubbs who had missed the United game with a hamstring strain was back in training days before the final. There was a slight question mark over Paul Lambert, who had been substituted against United, but it looked as if he would be able to play in at least some part of the game. The only real selection headache that Jansen had was the manager's favourite bugbear of who to leave out. Andy Thom had played himself back into contention with two goals against United the previous Saturday to cap a devastatingly effective display, Darren Jackson was also fit enough to give him attacking options and Rico Annoni had been playing well in defence whenever he was called on. There was speculation that Jansen would leave out Regi Blinker, whose poor form had hit a low in the league match against United, and possibly revert to a four-man midfield with Lambert getting the nod in favour of Wieghorst. In the end Jansen went for a four-man midfield with Wieghorst, in what turned out to be a decisive move, and Thom and Blinker played in a three-man attack at the expense of Simon Donnelly.

For those who believe in such things, the omens for Dundee United were not encouraging. For one thing they had never beaten Celtic in a cup final; in addition this would be their twenty-third meeting in all stages of the tournament and Celtic had lost only four times. Add to that 2–1 and 4–0 defeats in the league – the most recent only eight days previously – and things did not look good for the Tannadice side. On the other hand, Dundee United fans could console themselves with the knowledge that the form book tends to go out of the window in cup finals, as Celtic certainly knew, and they could not possibly surrender as meekly as they had the previous week. Unfortunately for the United fans they were spectacularly wrong on both counts.

The comprehensive manner of Celtic's total domination of this game virtually ended it as a contest from the moment Jim McCluskey blew his whistle to start the match. Celtic were in complete control. United, who had sat back for the first half hour in the league game, this time merely seemed paralysed either by fear or the sense of the big occasion. They attempted to smother the game but, in the process, conceded acres of space to Celtic which, when Henrik Larsson is playing, amounts to the footballing equivalent of a suicide note. But although Larsson was frequently given enough room to drive a bus through the United defence, it was his fellow Scandinavian Morten Wieghorst who was having possibly his best game in a Celtic shirt. Jansen had cast Wieghorst in a new midfield role and the Dane was revelling in being able to surge forward in support of the attack with his strong running. Celtic were so much in command that a goal was inevitable.

The move started on the left with Blinker, who was having a comfortable if unspectacular game, and the fans, sensing his anxiety, were doing their best to settle him. With the left channel blocked, Blinker passed to McNamara in the middle of the field who quickly switched it to Andy Thom. By this stage Wieghorst was going like a train on the right-hand side, Thom looked up and saw him before delivering a perfect ball at his feet. Without hesitation Wieghorst whipped the ball into the United box where Rieper rose unhindered to

Marc Rieper celebrates after putting Celtic one up in the final

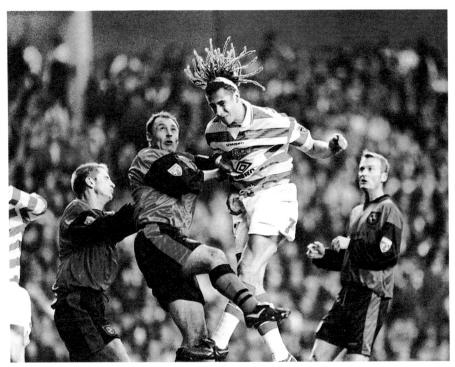

Henrik Larsson was a constant torment to the Dundee United defence

head past Dykstra. With 20 minutes gone Celtic were a goal ahead.

Four minutes later the game was effectively over as a contest. In their two league encounters so far this season Dundee United had yet to effectively counter the threat of Henrik Larsson. Whenever the Swede ran at them, the United defence invariably backed off or stood stock-still. This time they were backing off. Larsson had gathered the ball about 35 yards out, shaping for a shot as the United defenders back-tracked. As Larsson shot, veteran defender Maurice Malpas stuck out a leg and the ball took a slight deflection and sailed into the net leaving Dykstra helpless.

Dundee United had been unable to raise their game and never looked like overcoming a two-goal deficit. Even so, the manner in which they ran up the white flag must have been hugely disappointing to their fans. The United attack was so ineffectual that it was 78 minutes before they had a shot on target. That was a testament to a Celtic defence which had been so effective in this tournament it had not

Craig Burley stumbles but the ball is already in the net for Celtic's third

conceded a single goal in five games. United's single shot came from Robbie Winters and Gould dealt with it comfortably, but by that time they were trailing 3–0 and the game was well beyond them. In 58 minutes Craig Burley had sealed United's fate thanks, once again, to that man Wieghorst. It was Wieghorst who picked up the ball in the middle of the park before slipping it to Larsson. Looking around for support, Larsson waited for Blinker to arrive before firing a pass out to the left. Blinker gathered the ball, rounded two defenders and then crossed for Burley to outjump two United defenders and head the ball in at the near post.

Burley's goal signalled the start of party time for the huge Celtic support. The songs and chants rolled off the Ibrox terracings and onto the pitch. Obviously they had some effect because as the fans chanted 'Rico, Rico', Jansen, who had given Paul Lambert a run out a minute earlier, gave them their wish and sent the charismatic Italian on with

A triumphant Tom Boyd with the Coca-Cola Cup

only a minute to go. When the Cup was presented Annoni's celebrations were almost as entertaining as the game itself. He had hardly touched the ball, but anyone would have thought he'd scored a hat-trick and not a single Celtic fan grudged him a moment of his delight. The fans joined in with their newly adopted anthem – 'Roll With It' by Oasis – as the players bedecked in scarves, baseball caps, Harpo wigs and anything else they could scavenge from the thousands thrown onto the pitch began a celebration which would not end for many hours to come.

Later Wim Jansen and the fans would reflect that the Coca-Cola Cup was no longer the tournament it once was. There was now no automatic European qualification for instance, but a trophy was still a trophy and it was the first addition to the Celtic silverware

The first trophy is in the bag and the happy faces say it all

Above: *Morten Wieghorst with his Man of the Match award*

Right: *Proud dad Jonathan Gould with his three-year-old son Matthew and a rather handsome piece of silverware*

A smiling Wim Jansen prepares for his post-match press interviews

Celtic's Cup final hit-men: Larsson, Burley and Rieper

since the Scottish Cup in May 1995. But it augured well for a team which had come a long way in a short time.

'Winning the Coca-Cola Cup is a start and we will see where that takes us,' said Wim Jansen. 'The most important thing about the win was that we played as a team. We were confident and if we show those attributes each time we step out on the field then, who knows?'

Celtic 3   Dundee United 0
Rieper
Larsson
Burley

Celtic: Gould, Rieper, Stubbs, Boyd, McNamara, Burley, Wieghorst, Mahé, Thom, Larsson, Blinker

Substitutes: Donnelly for Thom, Lambert for Blinker, Annoni for McNamara

Bookings: None

Attendance: 49,305

Above: *A happy Larsson with the Coca-Cola Cup*

Left: *Fergus McCann with the Coca-Cola Cup*

A job well done: the players applaud the fans after the final

THE GAP WIDENS

Kilmarnock v Celtic
6 December 1997

By another of those strange quirks of the fixture list Celtic's next game after winning the Coca-Cola Cup was a battle of the Cup-holders. They would go to Rugby Park to face Scottish Cup winners Kilmarnock, but any notions of some kind of 'super-Cup' match were quickly knocked on the head by the sort of game which could get football outlawed.

This was a battle of a strong midfield against a rigid defence and both goalkeepers might as well have spared themselves the December chill and sat in the stand for all the work they had to do. It would be easy to dismiss this Celtic performance as a Cup hangover but, even if they might have been allowed to be a little flat, it was a game they should certainly have won. After all, they had met – and won against – Kilmarnock only days after their exertions against Liverpool at Anfield, which should also have been a hangover moment. On that occasion, however, Celtic raised their game for 20 minutes and rattled in four goals.

There would be no goals in this game, which served once again to highlight Celtic's lack of a striker. Jock Brown was on record as saying that they were casting the net far and wide for a striker to fit Jansen's requirements. On the other hand, he pointed out whoever they signed would have to be better than Larsson, Donnelly or Jackson, internationals all. Jackson, however, had been ill for most of the season, Larsson was not a natural striker and preferred to play behind a front man, while Donnelly still required some seasoning before he could lead the line with confidence week in and week out. What Celtic really needed was a natural penalty-box predator, a man who could take half-chances in the six-yard box and turn them into goals. A man indeed like the late lamented – by the fans if not the management – Jorge Cadete, who could create goals out of nothing. To be fair to Brown, quality strikers are not exactly thick on the ground and although the search would be concluded soon, it would not be soon enough for the Kilmarnock game.

This one from Rieper went wide as Celtic stumbled to a 0–0 draw at Kilmarnock

Simon Donnelly failed to break the deadlock in Celtic's Coca-Cola hangover

On balance though, it is debatable whether Ronaldo himself could have fashioned much out of this game. With no real cutting edge up front, Celtic were also denied the services of Wieghorst and Blinker through suspension. Ironically, this was immediately after both men had played their best games in Celtic shirts in the final against Dundee United. With Blinker and Wieghorst out of the equation the supply lines to the Celtic forwards were somewhat choked. Kilmarnock were content to pack their defence and let Celtic simply pound away at them.

Thom had a shot blocked in a packed penalty box, then had one saved easily by Lekovic. The Kilmarnock keeper also blocked a shot from Donnelly and then saved a long-range effort from Stubbs at the second attempt. This was really the Killie keeper's only contribution to an afternoon which saw Celtic shoot wide, shoot high and, in some cases, not shoot at all. Celtic managed six shots on target in the whole of the game. At the other end Jonathan Gould had even less to do as Kilmarnock didn't manage a single shot on target. Kilmarnock were in the Celtic area often enough to have three penalty claims turned down, but the Celtic keeper scarcely had a save to make. Paul Wright shot off target, a Nevin cross was neatly dealt with by Rieper, then Nevin himself missed the best chance of the game when he headed past with the whole goal to choose from.

This was dour stuff and the only highlight for Celtic came in the play of Paul Lambert who was fully fit and settling into the rigours of the Scottish game. Lambert showed the defensive midfield qualities for which he had been signed and, in the absence of Wieghorst and Blinker, he was able to link with Donnelly to set up what few chances there were. It was a dismal game and, undoubtedly, the home fans were the happier when the referee put everyone out of their misery by blowing for full time.

While Celtic had been toiling, Hearts had won comfortably and Rangers would pick up three points against Hibs the following day. The combination of results left Celtic still in third place in the league – seven points behind the Edinburgh side and six points behind Rangers. Celtic had a game in hand over Rangers, but they had played the same number of games as Hearts. The seven-point gap was beginning to get troublesome and with the two sides due to meet inside a week the game was beginning to take on massive significance.

By the time Celtic and Hearts met at Celtic Park the following Saturday, Celtic would have been bolstered by the arrival of a man that Jansen described as the final piece in the jigsaw. On top of that there was a welcome return to scoring form which would cap one of the season's most remarkable comebacks. But before they could even think about Hearts there was still the question of Aberdeen at Pittodrie in a mere three days.

Celtic 0   Kilmarnock 0

Celtic: Gould, Rieper, Stubbs, Boyd, McNamara, Burley, Lambert, Mahé, Donnelly, Larsson, Thom

Substitutes: Jackson for Thom

Bookings: Lambert, Boyd, Mahé

Attendance: 15,632

BACK IN BUSINESS

Aberdeen v Celtic
9 December 1997

No one connected with Celtic Park, whether it be Wim Jansen, his players, the officials and especially not the fans, was in any doubt that it was important to get back into a winning routine and quickly. The Coca-Cola Cup was already in the trophy cabinet but in the scheme of things it didn't count for much; the trophy plus a third-place finish in the league would get you into Europe. Celtic had bigger fish to fry. They had the championship in mind and their form of late had been far from satisfactory. They had won only one of their past five league games and that against a Dundee United side which caved in without too much pressure. More importantly, in three of those five games they had failed to score. Suddenly the defence was starting to leak goals and the forwards were losing their touch.

The solution to the scoring problem had been a vexing situation for Wim Jansen. The man he wanted was Harald Brattbakk of Rosenborg but, like Paul Lambert before him, the Norwegian was tied up in the Champions League. Celtic had been talking to Brattbakk for some time and he had already visited Glasgow twice in the past six weeks. Brattbakk was keen to come but, with nine Champions League goals to his credit and 14 goals overall in European competition, Rosenborg were reluctant to let him go, especially since they had an outside chance of qualifying for the quarter-finals of the Champions League themselves. Eventually, however, a pre-contract agreement was signed which would make Brattbakk a Celtic player until the year 2002. For their part, Rosenborg agreed that he could leave the day after their final Champions Cup sectional tie. That game was on Wednesday, 10 December, which would mean he could be in Glasgow to face Hearts in the vital league game the following Saturday. Before that, however,

Celtic would have to find a solution to their striking problem against Aberdeen.

Aberdeen were in the middle of a dismal run of form, but Pittodrie on a cold Tuesday night was still no place to go looking for points. The Dons were invariably capable of making life difficult for Celtic and, even though Aberdeen had not won in their last ten meetings, Celtic knew they would have a game on their hands. Celtic would again be without the increasingly influential Morten Wieghorst, who was serving the final game of a two-game ban, but Wim Jansen was still able to spring a surprise on the thousands of Celtic fans who had made the trip north for the game. Darren Jackson was starting a game for the first time since 23 August.

The final piece of the jigsaw: Harald Brattbakk arrives from Rosenborg

Jackson's illness had shaken Scottish football and there were those who wondered if he would ever play again, far less return this season. Fortunately, Jackson was not among that number. After his surgery in August he astonished his doctors, and his team-mates, with the speed of his recovery. By September he was back in light training; the following month he resumed full training; and in November he made a comeback in a reserve game at Ross County. Any doubts about his encephalitis affecting his courage were quickly dispelled when, within minutes of the game starting, Jackson got underneath a ball – which was coming down with snow on it – and headed it with no ill effects. His re-appearance in the first team came as a substitute in that 1–1 draw against Rangers and, even though he missed the Coca-Cola Cup final, he was now able to come on from the start. Jackson's return to the team came at just the right time because he knew that with the imminent arrival of Brattbakk he would have to fight hard to re-establish himself. What he didn't know was that over the coming weeks he and Brattbakk would effectively share the same jersey at Celtic Park.

Aberdeen were the perfect opposition for Jackson's comeback. They were coached by his old Hibs manager Alex Miller and in his first game against his old boss Jackson was hoping to contribute to a thoroughly miserable time for his former gaffer. Jackson found himself playing behind Larsson, who was being used as a solo striker, as Jansen fielded an unusual 3-5-1-1. Jansen plainly expected Aberdeen to come at Celtic and he had fashioned a team which could control the midfield and hit explosively on the break. Certainly, it was the home side who started as though their careers were depending on the result. The Celtic defence found themselves earning their corn as Aberdeen piled on the pressure early on. Billy Dodds came close in 11 minutes with a neat chip which Stubbs had to clear off the line. Between them, Stubbs and Jonathan Gould were at full stretch to keep Aberdeen at bay. Gould had become used to making vital saves late on in the game when his concentration needed to be pin-sharp, but here he found himself under siege straight from the off. Two marvellous saves, both from Stephen Glass, kept Celtic in the game and slowly began to convince Aberdeen that it might not be their night.

Having weathered the early storm, Celtic began to put their foot on the ball and used the extra man in midfield to good effect. The tide of the game began to turn in their favour as they began to put Jim Leighton under pressure in the Aberdeen goal. Jackson, who was looking sharp, was first to trouble the keeper with a snap-shot from about 15 yards out, which Leighton did well to stop on the line. The attacks were all coming from Celtic now and it was not long before they drew first blood. Regi Blinker sent a long ball down the left-hand channel to Stephane Mahé. The French defender had now settled in to his role and was becoming more adventurous and more effective in his overlapping runs. Mahé ran on to the ball from Blinker and took it to within a few yards of the by-line before firing in a shot which Leighton had to dive full length to reach. Although he got to it, Leighton was not able to get both hands to it, he could only punch it away and watch with

Left: *Darren Jackson back in training only weeks after his life-threatening illness*

Below: *Darren Jackson capped his comeback with a goal in the 2–0 defeat of Aberdeen at Pittodrie*

Stephane Mahe in action against Aberdeen in the 2–0 win at Celtic Park

horror as it landed in front of Henrik Larsson who smashed it into the net past the prone Leighton. Celtic were a goal ahead with 40 minutes on the clock.

Celtic had started the game sluggishly but had come into it more as the first half wore on. They began the second half in a similar fashion to the way they had ended the first and Aberdeen were put under constant pressure. For long periods of the game the red-shirted players were simply pinned in their own half. When they got the ball out they could not do anything with it as the Celtic defence, perhaps chastened by those early scares, put the shutters up. There was always going to be at least one more goal in this game and when it came no one could deny the justice of the scorer's cause. Skipper Tom Boyd picked up the ball in the centre circle with half the field stretching before him. He spotted

Blinker making a run on his right and gave the ball to the Dutchman, who didn't have a defender near him. Blinker, who hadn't had much success in shooting so far, continued his run carrying the ball to the edge of the Aberdeen area before unleashing a shot himself. Once again Leighton was equal to it and managed to stop it, but once again he was unable to hold it. This time the ball fell at the feet of Darren Jackson who had the presence of mind to knock it wide of the sprawling keeper and stroke it into the net.

No one was happier than Darren Jackson. First he ran to the Celtic fans to the right of Leighton's goal and was swamped by a crowd of bodies which threatened to drag him into the terracings. Then he broke free and ran to embrace his team-mates. The look on Jackson's face as he screamed 'I'm back, I'm back', to the Celtic dugout was enough to warm the heart of any Scottish football fan.

Afterwards, with the three points safely in the bag, Jackson reflected that he had been fortunate to have an understanding referee who had not booked him for leaping into the crowd. But even though he had scored a fairy-tale goal, Jackson was keeping things in perspective.

'It was a dream return for me, and it was great to get the goal,' he said. 'But the most important thing was the three points we picked up.'

Celtic 2   Aberdeen 0
Larsson
Jackson

Celtic: Gould, Stubbs, Rieper, Boyd, Blinker, Mahé, Burley, Lambert, McNamara, Jackson, Larsson

Substitutes: Donnelly for Jackson

Bookings: None

Attendance: 16,981

THE CUTTING EDGE

Hearts v Celtic
13 December 1997

One of the first calls that Jock Brown received shortly after Celtic had beaten Aberdeen was from Harald Brattbakk. The Norwegian striker was due at Celtic Park within 48 hours, but even in the middle of preparations for his final Champions League match he went out of his way to take the time to find out how his new club had got on. He also enquired after Darren Jackson, whose recovery had been dramatic enough to interest the Norwegian media, and was delighted to hear that he had scored.

Two days later Jackson and Brattbakk were able to meet when the 26-year-old Norwegian was introduced to his new team-mates. Brattbakk had seen the ground before and been impressed, this time he was also impressed with the players he would be playing alongside.

'I can sense that here it is not just about 11 men,' he said. 'It is about a whole club and Celtic want to get better and that is something I want to be part of.'

When Brattbakk was paraded before the media, Wim Jansen described him as the final piece of the jigsaw. Despite his somewhat ascetic look and the rimless spectacles, the man who was a loan-broker in Norway's part-time footballing regime was billed as the man who would give Jansen's side the cutting edge which had been missing in recent weeks. Certainly Brattbakk's record would seem to bear out that billing. He had regularly been top scorer in the Norwegian championship and his strike rate of 127 goals in 148 games made impressive reading. Significantly, lest we thought he was the sort of player who scored for fun, Brattbakk did point out that one of the reasons he wanted to play in Scotland was to match himself against a better class of defender.

'I won't worry about the expectations,' he said of the burden which was awaiting him. 'After all it's only football and if I started to think about it things would only get worse. I do feel the big responsibility but if I give 100 per cent then I can't do any more – but I did it with Rosenborg and I will do it with Celtic. From what I've seen of Scottish football every team creates plenty of scoring chances, and I feel that if I get in on any of these then I will score. But the responsibility and the onus is on me to play well as part of the team first of all and then score goals.'

Brattbakk's midweek phone call to Jock Brown would have given him the welcome news that while Celtic had picked up three points against Aberdeen, Hearts had dropped a couple of points in their draw at Dundee United. The title race was now shaping into a three-way contest between Celtic, Rangers and Hearts. There were those who were still predicting that the Tynecastle bubble would burst and the next ten days would go a long way to determining the fortunes of both clubs. Celtic faced Hearts

Harald Brattbakk made his first appearance for the Hoops as a sub against Hearts

at home on the Saturday in a game which had the air of a good old-fashioned six-pointer about it. Then, the following week, while Celtic entertained Hibs, Hearts had to take on Rangers at Tynecastle. If results on both weekends went the right way Celtic, despite their poor spell in November, could actually be top of the league again.

Harald Brattbakk had arrived at Celtic Park in time to be considered for the game against Hearts and was immediately included in Wim Jansen's plans. Certainly the fans were eager to see the man about whom they had been promised so much, but it would be unreasonable to expect him to be on from the start. It seemed likely, though, that he would play a significant part of the game. In the end Brattbakk was named among the substitutes but nonetheless received a rousing reception from the terraces when he ran out in his green and white training livery for the warm-up. Jansen had a full-strength squad to choose from and for a game of this importance he had no hesitation in fielding what was coming to be recognised as his best team.

The four-man midfield of Lambert, Burley, Wieghorst and McNamara were firing on all cylinders in a game which Celtic dominated from the start. The match at Tynecastle had been a game which Celtic quickly took control of as Hearts failed to compete, and so it was here. The Celtic Park side were in charge from the first whistle and chance after chance rained in on Gilles Rousset's goal. It is a testament to the team which Jim Jefferies had fashioned that Hearts were still on level terms at half-time – any other team would have been at least a couple of goals down as the Celtic midfield ran riot. It emerged at half-time that Celtic's superiority had not been achieved without a price. The fans knew that Marc Rieper had been injured; he had been replaced by Annoni in 24 minutes after suffering a calf strain. What they did not know was that Henrik Larsson, who had become increasingly influential, had pulled a muscle and was in some doubt for the second half. Also, Stephane Mahé was battling on with a groin strain which he had picked up. After discussions between Jansen and Larsson it was decided that the Swede would go out for the second half and last as long as he could.

It was a remarkably prescient decision because it was Larsson who was responsible for creating the biggest roar of the game in 79 minutes.

*Alan Stubbs requires treatment as Celtic beat Hearts
2–1 at Tynecastle during their October clash*

*Stephane Mahe's short-lived Mohawk hairstyle made him look even
more fearsome*

Marc Rieper scores his first goal for Celtic to give them the lead
against Hearts in October, this time Celtic weren't so prolific

Although fans had become used to his blistering pace, it is easy to forget
that Larsson also has great physical strength, as Alan McManus found
out to his cost. Larsson had taken the ball to the goal line on the left-

hand side of the box with McManus at his shoulder. The Swede charged him out of the way, turned him, slipped, regained his composure, turned McManus again and then fired a deep cross towards the back post. Burley trapped the ball superbly, allowed it to fall at his feet and bounce, before hitting an unstoppable half-volley past Rousset. Celtic were a goal up when everyone knew that a lead of three or four goals would not have flattered them. Larsson, having done the damage, was immediately substituted before he could succumb to his injury. The fans, who had been becoming increasingly frustrated, began to sing and dance with delight the moment Burley's shot hit the net.

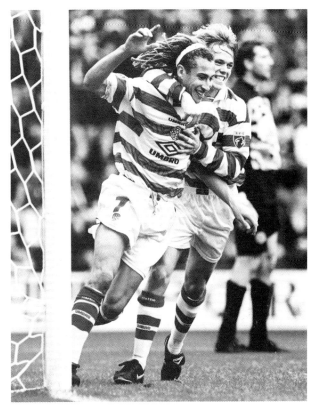

Larsson and Donnelly celebrate the Tynecastle win, Celtic's toughest league test so far

They had already been celebrating in 59 minutes when Brattbakk made his eagerly anticipated debut as a replacement for Regi Blinker who, to be kind, was having the sort of game he could only have in his worst nightmares. The roar which greeted his arrival was as bizarre as it was rousing. This was a man about whom the Celtic support knew little, but so desperate were they to see a striker of his reputation that his run on to the bench was greeted like the Second Coming. The only way anyone could possibly live up to the expectation implicit in that welcome would be to come off the bench and score a match-winning hat-trick. Brattbakk did not do that, but he showed he did have electrifying pace and would not shirk from getting into the tackles and tracking back where necessary.

Brattbakk did not score on his debut but, as he said himself, Celtic were a team where the goals tended to be spread around. Burley's goal

Almost inevitably, Henrik Larsson scores against Hearts, but that was back in October. This time Burley slots home the winner

– which turned out to be the match-winner – was his seventh of the season, which is an impressive haul for a midfielder. The Celtic fans left the ground delirious, not only because they had put a dent in Hearts' title aspirations, but also at the news that Rangers had only managed a goalless draw at Dunfermline.

Perhaps Santa would be wearing green and white this year after all.

Celtic 1   Hearts 0
Burley

Celtic: Gould, Boyd, Stubbs, Rieper, Mahé, McNamara, Burley, Lambert, Wieghorst, Larsson, Blinker

Substitutes: Annoni for Rieper, Brattbakk for Blinker, Jackson for Larsson

Bookings: None

Attendance: 50,035

REVENGE

Hibs v Celtic
20 December 1997

In the days after the win over Hearts, Celtic fans were indulging in their own brand of fantasy football. By dropping points at Dunfermline, Rangers had thrown the championship race wide open and, not for the first time, there was every chance of Celtic going to the top of the league. Calculator salesmen would do a roaring trade over the next few months as the top three swapped places on a number of occasions. But, with Celtic at home to Hibs and Hearts at home to Rangers, there is no doubt that this was one of the key Saturdays in the season. By the time those who had managed to avoid shopping duty on that last Saturday before Christmas poured into the ground, they knew what was required of their team. The perfect result would be a goalless draw at Tynecastle between Hearts and Rangers which would then allow Celtic to go top on goal difference if they could beat Hibs by three goals.

This was indeed the stuff of fantasy and played little part in the thinking in the Celtic dressing-room. The view there was that they were capable of beating anyone, and if they did that from now to the end of the season then the league would be theirs without any need to resort to goal difference. Before that though, there was the small matter of having to beat Hibs, the side who had contributed to Celtic's shocking start to the season with that 2–1 first-day defeat at Easter Road. Since then, the fortunes of the two clubs could not have been more different. Celtic had dragged themselves up by their bootstraps and meshed as a cohesive unit which was mounting its most serious championship challenge in years – while Hibs, who had promised much at the start of the season, were now second bottom of the division with only three wins from 17 games.

A lot had changed at Celtic in the 16 games between the two

fixtures. Five of the side who had played in the opening game – Gordon Marshall, Tosh McKinlay, Malky Mackay, Tommy Johnson and Andreas Thom – were no longer key elements in the Jansen plan. The new faces who had replaced them, however, had not forgotten what had happened in that opening game and were determined that revenge would have to be taken on the Edinburgh side. Whatever the outcome, it would have to be determined without Marc Rieper and Stephane Mahé. The Danish international had limped off after 24 minutes against Hearts and, despite intensive treatment from physio Brian Scott, his calf injury did not clear up in time to play Hibs. This meant another place in the starting line up for Rico Annoni, who seemed to have accepted his new role as spare defender filling in for either Rieper or Stubbs when the occasion demanded. Mahé was still troubled by a groin strain he had picked up against Hearts and that meant a game in defence for David Hannah. Up front there was still no starting place for Harald Brattbakk, who was being given some time to acclimatise to the demands of the Scottish game.

Despite the obvious desire for revenge among the Celtic camp, for a few horrible moments in the first half it looked like – as the great baseball sage Yogi Berra once said – déjà vu all over again. It was Celtic who found themselves defending doggedly against some persistent Hibs attacks. Gould caused a few flutters among the Celtic fans when he made an uncharacteristic hash of a couple of early corners. Fortunately, his defenders were up to the job and the Hibs forwards were not up to theirs. Fifteen minutes into the game Gould was again in action when he had to race out to block a shot from Andy Dow, who smashed the ball against the keeper when it seemed easier to score.

Celtic had plainly had enough and it was time to kick in to a higher gear. Craig Burley, who had been criticised because his form had allegedly shaded, shook the game into life for the Celtic fans with his eighth goal of the season. The goal came from a typical McNamara run down the right and when he cut the ball back, Burley came steaming through the middle to smack the ball home. Celtic took complete control of the game and went further ahead five minutes before half-time when Wieghorst headed in a Blinker corner.

The manner in which Blinker was received by the Celtic fans was one of the more heartening aspects of this match. Blinker had had, on his own admission, probably his worst game in a Celtic shirt the previous Saturday against Hearts. This was followed by newspaper quotes which appeared to suggest that the Dutch winger was arrogantly lashing out at the fans for booing him. Blinker claimed that he had been misquoted when all he had been trying to say was that he had been giving 100 per cent and didn't know what else to do. Whatever he had said, or tried to say, the result was that the fans got behind Blinker and every touch against Hibs was cheered to the echo. As a consequence Blinker had one of his better games and was instrumental in the Hibs downfall.

Having set up the second goal five minutes before half-time, Blinker then played his part in the third. A minute after the restart he switched play from left to right with a long perfectly weighted ball to Jackie McNamara, which the young wing-back gratefully smashed past Reid and into the net. This was the three-goal cushion that the mathematically inclined Celtic fans had been looking for, but unfortunately Hearts were losing and losing heavily against Rangers so the sums came to nothing. Celtic, however, were rampant and Blinker was having a great day. In 64 minutes he played his part in Celtic's fourth goal. Blinker chipped the ball into the Hibs penalty box, but it was too far in front of Henrik Larsson. The ball bounced between keeper Chris Reid and Hibs defender John Hughes but neither of them moved for it. Larsson saw his chance, kept his run going and nipped in between them to stick the ball into the net. It was a combination of opportunism and sheer cheek, but no one at Celtic was complaining.

A couple of minutes later Brattbakk made his second appearance in a Celtic jersey when he again came on as a substitute, this time for Wieghorst. As he had been the week before, the Norwegian was full of running without actually getting his name on the score sheet. That final honour went once again to Craig Burley who had started the rout so he decided to finish it. Celtic kept the best till last with a goal in the ninetieth minute to take the breath away. Thom, who had also come on as a substitute, took a short corner out on the right and from fully 30 yards Burley hammered it beyond Chris Reid and into the net.

The fans were ecstatic as Celtic notched up their most comprehensive win of the season, in a performance which augured well for the second half of the campaign. Rangers had also scored five against Hearts in a remarkable 5–2 scoreline which thwarted any hopes of Celtic topping the league again. But as the crowds streamed home from the East End of Glasgow that Christmas Saturday, no one could convince them that it would be long until they did.

Celtic 5   Hibs 0
Burley (2)
Wieghorst
Larsson
McNamara

Celtic: Gould, Hannah, Stubbs, Annoni, Boyd, Lambert, Burley, Wieghorst, McNamara, Larsson, Blinker

Substitutes: Brattbakk for Wieghorst, Jackson for Larsson, Thom for Blinker

Bookings: Burley

Attendance: 49,094

A CHRISTMAS STUFFING

St Johnstone v Celtic
27 December 1997

The game against Hibs brought Celtic to the halfway point of their season. With 18 games gone, the season – which had begun ignominiously against the Edinburgh side – was looking considerably brighter. Rangers, to be sure, were top of the league, but only by a single point from Celtic. Ominously for both clubs Hearts, who had taken a solitary point from three tough games, were still only a point behind Celtic. It was shaping up to be the most competitive championship race Scotland had seen for years.

There was no overdoing the turkey and trimmings for Wim Jansen's side over Christmas. They would travel to Perth to face St Johnstone on 27 December in a repeat of the fixture which was responsible for turning their season around back in August. Celtic had played St Johnstone three times already and had notched up an aggregate score of 5–0 and no one really expected that pattern to be altered in any way in this game. There would be no Christmas boxes handed out by Celtic to deserving St Johnstone players – at least that was the theory. The alarm bells should perhaps have started ringing when Jansen named his team. Marc Rieper's calf injury was still improving slowly and Stephane Mahé was almost at full fitness, but neither man was able to take part in the match. This meant another outing for their deputies in the shape of Annoni and Hannah. More ominously for Celtic there was no Henrik Larsson, also because of injury. The midfield engine-room partnership of Burley and Lambert could still look a little tentative at times, although it was nearing the finished article. However, there was no doubt for Celtic that Larsson had become their most influential player over the past few weeks. When Larsson played, Celtic played, and the stocky striker's darting runs into space gave Celtic so many attacking options. Larsson was always there for the one-two, to leave the defender for dead with an adrenaline surge of pace, to exploit the hesitancy of opposing keepers and simply to stick them away with devastating accuracy. Larsson had scored 15 goals and made countless others in his 26 appearances so far.

What was perhaps more surprising was the fact that in the absence of the man who was far and away his top goalscorer, Jansen also continued to ignore the 'cutting edge' of his team. Once again Harald Brattbakk, the man the club had tracked for months and forked out a lot of money to bring to Celtic Park, would start the game on the bench. Jansen went into this game with a striking combination of Regi Blinker and Darren Jackson with Simon Donnelly, like Brattbakk, cooling his heels on the bench.

Even so, the fans would have reckoned the team that Jansen sent out should have been well capable of beating St Johnstone. But if the alarm bells did not ring when the team was announced over the McDiarmid Park PA system, they certainly started ringing the moment the game began. The thousands of fans who had made the trip up the motorway to Perth watched in horror as the team served up what may have been the worst Celtic performance of the past year. Celtic played as if they had only been introduced to each other on the coach. Every team can expect to have one, or possibly two players having an off day, but to have six or seven is an almost insurmountable problem. Jonathan Gould, who was aiming for his sixth straight clean sheet, was going to have to put in a hard shift if he was to maintain his record.

It was Gould, indeed, who was in action straight away. McDiarmid Park had been the scene of his match-altering save against George O'Boyle back at the start of the season. With less than two minutes on the clock, he and O'Boyle were renewing hostilities when the striker let fly with a 25-yard drive which Gould did well to stop. Gould was again in action later in the half with another fine save from Calum Davidson. Remarkably, Gould was keeping his side in the game. Celtic were playing as though the 15 matches since their last visit to McDiarmid Park had never happened. They were at sixes and sevens throughout the game and being physically bossed around by a St Johnstone side which tackled tigerishly and hustled the Celtic players at every opportunity.

Celtic, for their part, were desperately missing their injured trio. Without Rieper, Stubbs was limited in his opportunities to come forward but, more importantly, without the vision and ingenuity of Larsson there was no one to see the gaps and put St Johnstone under pressure.

Celtic managed a single cohesive attacking move in the first half when McNamara and Wieghorst combined, but they seldom troubled the Saints defence. Whatever Jansen said at half-time didn't do much to turn things around. He persisted with the same 11 in the second half, when it might have been more prudent to substitute Blinker who was doing his confidence no good in an unusual striking role. Still Brattbakk and Donnelly stayed on the bench and still Celtic failed to pose any real threat. Craig Burley did have a header cleared off the line, but that was as close as they came. One of the most frequent criticisms of Jansen from the Celtic fans was his often bizarre use of substitutes: players who were playing poorly were often left on, while more blameless ones were substituted. On other occasions the substitution came too late to make any material difference. Against St Johnstone Jansen made his first substitution early enough when Brattbakk came on in 63 minutes, but, bizarrely, it was for Jackson rather than Blinker – whose personal purgatory was allowed to continue. Brattbakk added some strong running to the Celtic side but he too missed the linking play of Larsson and had nothing to run on to.

The way Celtic were playing an upset was always on the cards and it came in 72 minutes. Appropriately, it was a goal which shared all the qualities of the game; it was messy, awkward and horrible to watch. The goal came from an Alan Preston cross on the right which disappeared into a mob of players. With the Celtic goalmouth resembling a playground kickabout and Gould unsighted by a Saints player in front of him, O'Boyle stabbed out a leg and got a measure of revenge by forcing the ball over the line. McNamara did try to clear it with his arm, but since he himself was actually in the goal at the time it was a futile effort. Celtic were stunned, but Saints and their fans were jubilant. They had been put through the wringer three times by Celtic, now it was their turn.

Surprisingly, the goal did nothing to shake Celtic out of their lassitude and it wasn't until the very last minute of the game that they started hammering shots in on Alan Main. Even at this late stage Celtic had shots from Thom and Burley blocked, and even though they were never worth the draw, it was not beyond them until the referee blew for full time.

A game which had appeared to be a formality had turned out to be a nightmare. Not only that, Rangers had won and extended their lead to four points with the Ne'erday Old Firm fixture less than a week away. A plainly unhappy Wim Jansen refused to apportion blame for the defeat which was just as well since, with the possible exception of Gould, no one was blameless.

'You win as a team and you lose as a team,' he said tersely. 'It is not about one player. We had many who didn't perform at Perth.'

Jansen knew he had less than seven days to get them to perform or hand a seven-point advantage to their oldest rivals.

Celtic 0   St Johnstone 1
                          O'Boyle

Celtic: Gould, Hannah, Annoni, Stubbs, Boyd, McNamara, Burley, Wieghorst, Lambert, Blinker, Jackson

Substitutes: Brattbakk for Jackson, Thom for Stubbs

Bookings: Stubbs, Boyd

Attendance: 10,554

THE TURNING POINT?

Rangers v Celtic
2 January 1998

Since Enrico Annoni signed from AS Roma in March 1997, his Scottish sojourn had proved to be something of a mixed experience. He had been at Celtic Park less than a year and, as well as a long spell with injury, he had seemed to flit in and out of both Tommy Burns' and Wim Jansen's plans. Annoni had, however, quickly emerged as a fans' favourite. His uncompromising play and his enthusiasm for the game and the Celtic faithful had endeared him to the fans. The waves of 'Rico, Rico' washed down from the stands to break on the roof of the Celtic dugout when the crowd decided it was time for their boy to get an outing. Annoni had started only four games for Celtic so far this season, but he was about to play the game of his life.

Wim Jansen served his apprenticeship in the great Dutch World Cup side of the '70s, shoulder to shoulder with the genius of Cruyff and Neeskens. When he was appointed at Celtic Park no less a figure than Johann Cruyff himself delivered a glowing tribute to his tactical skills. The Celtic fans had already had an inkling of that in the way Jansen had changed their style of play and transformed 11 strangers – including eight new faces – into a team. But his shining hour, tactically, came in the traditional Ne'erday fixture against Rangers. The game now is never played on New Year's Day and this year battle would be joined at Celtic Park on 2 January. Jansen had been critical of his team against St Johnstone and he knew an entirely different approach would be needed against Rangers.

'I had tough decisions to make about who started and who didn't, but I made these taking into account the game situation,' said Jansen, who was going to have to make the most important team selection of his short career at Celtic.

One of the decisions which would have to be taken would be about Regi Blinker. The Dutchman had been off-form and, at times, Jansen had been accused of blind loyalty to his countryman, but on this occasion he made the tough decision and Blinker did not make the final 14. The other tough decision concerned Harald Brattbakk – he would start for the first time having been seasoned in his three appearances as a substitute. The defence was bolstered by the return of Marc Rieper to combine again with Alan Stubbs, but Stephane Mahé was still missing. This time Jansen preferred the vastly experienced Annoni to David Hannah in a three-man defence with Stubbs and Rieper. Jansen had learned a lot from the first two Old Firm games and for this match he decided to match Rangers head to head. For the first time in their three meetings the teams lined up in identical 3-5-2 formations. Jansen had one ace up his sleeve. Although Annoni was forming a back three with Rieper and Stubbs, he was also given special responsibility to mark Brian Laudrup. Like Larsson for Celtic, when Laudrup played, Rangers played, and if he could be stopped then the game might turn for Celtic. Annoni, who had been schooled in Serie A, where defence has become an art form, was the man for the job.

Rangers started the more brightly of the two sides and it took Celtic some moments to settle to their task. One early pivotal moment came in eight minutes when Stubbs clipped the heels of Laudrup as he ran across the 18-yard line. Television replays suggest that, despite his extravagant tumble, Laudrup was inside the box when the Celtic defender made contact, but referee Hugh Dallas didn't award the penalty. Eventually Rico Annoni settled to his task and Laudrup found himself being shadowed everywhere by Celtic's own Bald Eagle. Sure enough, without Laudrup Rangers were missing that vital spark and slowly Celtic started to come into the game. As well as the negation of Laudrup's influence, the wing play of Tom Boyd also started to take effect. Boyd was playing as a wing-back out on the right and he found a lot of space and got a lot of change out of the inexperienced Rino Gattuso. Slowly the game began to turn in Celtic's favour. Burley and Lambert seemed determined to make a nonsense of newspaper critics who said they couldn't play in the same midfield. While Lambert broke down the attacks, the ball could then be given to Burley to go forward in support of his attackers. With

Burley coming forward, Brattbakk could then be released on his darting runs. Twice the Norwegian found himself one-on-one with Goram, and the Rangers keeper had to be at his best to deny him.

Goram, indeed, was all that stood between Rangers and a considerable half-time deficit. Gould could have been sitting in the stand for all he had to do in the Celtic goal. During the half-time interval though, the pessimists among the Celtic fans were pointing out to anyone who would listen how they had seen all this before. How often had Goram broken their hearts? How often had Celtic played Rangers off the park? How often had they lost to a sloppy piece of defending?

Not this time.

The Celtic defence had been a little shaky in early November,

Burley scores the first goal against Rangers to break the Ne'erday hoodoo

but not now. With only one goal conceded in their last six league games, and that only the week before, parsimony was the order of the day in the Celtic defence. Celtic had been shaky at the start of the first half but there was no sign of nerves at the beginning of the second. They were in the ascendancy right from the start. Two minutes into the half, Goram had to fend off a Stubbs header, then he denied Brattbakk once again, before relying on a combination of the post and Alex Clelland's backside to keep out a Larsson shot. Celtic were completely in control, but still the Rangers defence held.

Then, in 65 minutes, came the moment that the home fans had been waiting for. The Rangers defence managed to break down another

*Stuart McCall can't get his tackle in on Craig
Burley . . .*

*. . . and Goram can't get a hand to it as Celtic go into the lead in the
second half*

Jackson and David Hannah celebrate Burley's goal from the bench

Celtic attack. The ball was cleared, but only as far as McNamara who then played a delightful reverse pass into the path of Craig Burley who sent a drive rocketing past Goram. Celtic were ahead and the roof almost came off. Rangers had no real reply to the goal. Celtic sat in and waited for the anticipated onslaught which simply never came. The Ibrox side were playing like Celtic in the first league clash, they simply did not compete. Walter Smith threw on Paul Gascoigne for Jorg Albertz in 72 minutes in the hope of turning the game back their way. Again, Jansen's tactical nous came to the fore. Within seconds of Gascoigne coming on, Jansen was at the touch-line detailing Lambert to pick him up. Among his many skills, Lambert is a superb man-marker and Gascoigne hardly got a kick of the ball.

Even at 1–0 ahead the Celtic fans would not be content. There was still 25 minutes to go and Celtic were defending a little too deep for the tastes of many of the fans. They would have preferred to see Rangers being held off a little closer to the halfway line. But still there was no great counter-attack from Rangers, they did not manage a single shot on goal for the whole game – a damning statistic. But, with five minutes to go, it all became academic. Darren Jackson had come on as

Harald Brattbakk gave Andy Goram a few anxious moments in the Norwegian's Old Firm debut

an eighty-fourth-minute replacement for Brattbakk who had run himself into the ground. Within a minute, Jackson unleashed one of his trademark curling drives from the edge of the box. Goram got to the shot but, once again, his defenders failed to clear the danger. This time the ball fell to Lambert who struck it superbly from 25 yards out and watched it rise all the way until it passed Goram, clipped an upright and then nestled in the top right-hand corner of Goram's net. It was 2–0 and the game was over.

Before this match there had been talk of all sorts of Celtic hoodoos. The number ten had taken on talismanic significance for both sets of fans. It had been ten years since Celtic won in this fixture; ten games since Rangers had lost in an Old Firm derby; and ten titles was the record which no team in Scotland had won in a row. Celtic's win smashed whatever jinx there might have been and made sure Rangers were not going to set a new record without a fight.

'The New Year's Day game was the most satisfying moment of my season,' says Alan Stubbs, who had been the Celtic hero in their last meeting with Rangers. 'I didn't know this at the time, but there was a tradition that whoever wins that game goes on to win the league and it proved to be the case with us.'

Celtic 2   Rangers 0
Burley
Lambert

Celtic: Gould, Rieper, Stubbs, Annoni, McNamara, Burley, Lambert,
    Wieghorst, Boyd, Larsson, Brattbakk

Substitutes: Jackson for Brattbakk

Bookings: Lambert, Boyd

Attendance: 49,350

Left: *Paul Lambert spared Celtic's blushes with a fine goal against his old club, Motherwell, as the two sides drew 1–1*

Below: *Harald Brattbakk had yet to score for Celtic and the draw at Motherwell left him still without a goal*

ALL IS NOT WELL

Motherwell v Celtic
10 January 1998

Their New Year win against Rangers put Celtic second in the table, just one point off the Ibrox club. They had been able to undo the damage they had done to themselves by losing at St Johnstone, and done Rangers some damage in the process. The two clubs had not been this close going into the second half of the season in years – ten years in fact. The last time Celtic had been within a point of Rangers was in the Centenary season in 1988 when they went on to win the title. With almost half the league programme still to be played there were those among the Celtic legions who were already entertaining notions of history repeating itself. Certainly, there was the tradition that whoever won the New Year game went on to win the league, but that probably had more to do with Rangers' dominance over the past nine years in this fixture and in the league itself, than with any tried and trusted statistical analysis.

At home, at least, Celtic were showing something close to championship form with only two defeats and one draw in 11 games. Their away form was another matter entirely. From their last four away matches they had managed only four points: a win against Aberdeen, a draw at Kilmarnock and defeats by Rangers and St Johnstone. This was far from satisfactory and was nowhere near the sort of form you would expect from putative champions. On Celtic's behalf, however, they frequently found life difficult away from home against teams who packed their defences and were desperate to gain even a point in front of their own fans. Celtic were also without the intimidatory effect of a 47,000-strong crowd when they went on the road. Even so, they had the skill and the personnel to break down defences and their away record was beginning to give cause for concern.

After the win against Rangers at Celtic Park, Celtic were away again the following weekend when they travelled to Fir Park to face Motherwell. The Lanarkshire side had already proved something of a handful in their two previous games. Celtic had the better of a five-goal thriller at Fir Park in September, but had been turned over 2–0 by Motherwell at Celtic Park in that dismal spell in November. Jansen had a full squad at his disposal, with Stephane Mahé and Phil O'Donnell both fully recovered. Mahé's return meant there was no place for Rico Annoni – despite his sterling efforts against Rangers – and, after being left out against Rangers, Regi Blinker was also included in the 14 at the expense of Simon Donnelly. Jansen abandoned the five-man midfield he had employed the previous week and went for four in the middle with three in attack. That meant that Harald Brattbakk would start for the second game in succession. The tall Norwegian was certain that the goals would come, but the fans were beginning to get a little impatient.

Sadly, it was obvious right from the start that the inconsistency which had dogged Celtic's season was coming into play once more. The players seemed drained by their heroics against Rangers when they had lifted themselves to such heights. Now, if not plumbing the depths, they were certainly wading out into pretty murky water. The players seemed uninspired as they moved through the first half without ever mentally getting out of third gear. That's not to say they did not have their moments. That first half saw ten Celtic corners as they pressed forward in search of the opening goal. Larsson, inevitably, came close, as did Mahé, who was coming forward more and more often in support of the attack. Motherwell had their moments too, but they were also apparently not in the mood to win a game that was really theirs for the taking.

The mood of the game changed dramatically ten minutes into the second half when Celtic found themselves a goal behind. Willie Falconer, who had been transferred to Motherwell from Celtic, did the damage with a fifty-fifth-minute header which spurred his old team into action. Six minutes later the scores were level again after Paul Lambert proved that lightning can strike twice. Eight days previously Lambert had been the toast of Celtic Park with a magnificent 25-yard strike which sealed the points against Rangers. Now he did again, this time from even further out. Lambert picked the ball up in the centre circle and laid it off to Wieghorst. As Lambert moved forward, the Dane completed the one-two and from fully 35 yards out Lambert hit a magnificent strike which left Woods repeating Goram's experience of watching the ball bury itself in the top corner of the net. With the scores level, Jansen took the opportunity to make changes. Brattbakk came off and Jackson came on in a pattern of substitution which would repeat itself so often in the remaining games the two men might as well have shared the same jersey.

Within minutes Celtic had their best chance of the game when Larsson burst into the penalty area only to be pulled down by Brian Martin, who had been paying close attention to him all afternoon. Referee Martin

The defensive partnership of Marc Rieper and Alan Stubbs would break the hearts of many an opposition manager in the championship-winning season

Clark had no hesitation in awarding the spot kick and, in the absence of regular penalty-taker Simon Donnelly, Darren Jackson volunteered. Jackson stepped up to take the kick, Woods went the wrong way but to the horror of the visiting fans Jackson shot wide.

Afterwards the striker would accept no excuses for his miss.

'People have said the penalty box was muddy and bumpy and that I had just come off the bench, but these didn't even come into it,' said Jackson. 'I was confident, but I have to hold my hands up to say that I committed the biggest sin of all in not hitting the target. If a goalkeeper saves a penalty then that is one thing, but missing the target altogether

Darren Jackson misses a penalty in a dour draw against Motherwell

is another. I had made my mind up which way I was putting the ball and the keeper went the wrong way but I missed.'

Jackson's missed penalty set the seal on a thoroughly miserable day for Celtic. It was an uninspired performance, but they could still have taken the three points. Instead, they had to settle for one – only their fifth in five away matches. This was a far cry from the team which went 14 games undefeated – including winning eight in a row – between August and October.

It was a problem which was becoming apparent to everyone, but especially to Wim Jansen.

'It is frustrating that we are not playing with the same authority away from home as, by and large, we have in games at Celtic Park,' he said. 'We appear to reserve our best football for games at our home ground, while in recent away matches we have allowed opponents to knock us off our stride and turn these games into physical battles.

'There is no reason why we shouldn't be able to perform as we did

Jackie McNamara in full cry – but the best Celtic could get was a share of the points

in the New Year game against Rangers when we go to play the likes of Motherwell and St Johnstone on their patch. That hasn't happened, but we must impress on players that it should be happening.'

Celtic 1   Motherwell 1
Lambert   Falconer

Celtic: Gould, Boyd, Stubbs, Rieper, Burley, Lambert, Wieghorst, Mahé, McNamara, Brattbakk, Larsson

Substitutes: Jackson for Brattbakk, Blinker for Wieghorst

Bookings: None

Attendance: 12,350

DOWN, BUT NOT OUT

Dundee United v Celtic
27 January 1998

In the midst of a dismal away run, Celtic managed to get a bit of a breather when their next league game, against Dundee United at Tannadice, was called off because of the weather. The timing was perfect, since it gave Celtic a chance to relax after a tough couple of weeks. The game would finally be played on Tuesday, 27 January, after Celtic's third-round Scottish Cup tie. The third round of the Scottish Cup is the surest sign that winter has us firmly in its grip, but the romance and adventure of the tournament can also bring a welcome respite from the winter chills. Celtic had been drawn at home against Greenock Morton and Wim Jansen put his Saturday off to good use by paying them the compliment of going down to Cappielow to personally scout the opposition when the United game was postponed.

Before the Cup tie, however, there were more changes in personnel with two long-serving players leaving the club. Andreas Thom had always made it clear that he would return to Germany after his spell with Celtic. The German's silky skills and dazzling runs had made him a firm favourite with the Celtic fans since he signed in July of 1995. However, with his contract about to run out and the player no longer figuring prominently in Wim Jansen's plans, he was allowed to move back to Germany and Hertha Berlin. Thom had made more than 100 appearances for Celtic – including 17 as a substitute – and had scored 27 goals, many of which would be remembered fondly by the fans. In the same week that Andy Thom left the club so too did Gordon Marshall. The affable keeper had signed for Celtic in the summer of 1991 and was the club's longest-serving professional. But with the stunning form of Jonathan Gould and the return to fitness of young Stewart Kerr he too, like Thom, had slipped out of the reckoning.

Marshall had played 136 times for Celtic and was too good a keeper to be left at number three in the pecking order, so the club accepted a bid from Kilmarnock to allow him to continue to play first-team football.

Celtic were about to bid farewell to another much-loved player, but this one would, thankfully, only be temporary. Tom Boyd was due to serve a three-game suspension after an accumulation of yellow cards. He could play against Morton but he would have to sit out potentially difficult league games against Dundee United, Aberdeen and Hearts.

Tom Boyd did turn out for Celtic against Morton in a side which seemed destined to make the football trivia books. Boyd and McNamara were the only two players in the starting 11 who had played in the tournament before – no fewer than nine Celtic players made their Scottish Cup debuts in the game against Morton. This showed the changes which Jansen had wrought in his first six months in charge. It was the most recent of those new faces – Harald Brattbakk – who settled two issues early in the game. The first was that he could score goals and the second was that Celtic were going to win. The game was only six minutes old when Stubbs, who was coming forward having left Rieper in defence, spotted Brattbakk making another of his diagonal runs. The defender laid the ball perfectly into the Norwegian's path for Brattbakk to slot the ball into the corner of the net without breaking stride.

Cup ties such as this are an occasion for smaller teams such as Morton to enjoy themselves and at the same time know that the club's financial problems have received a healthy boost. The Greenock side continued to make a game of it. They were not overawed in the slightest and they defended doggedly for the rest of the game. The second goal had to come and come it did when Jackson – who had come on for

Brattbakk celebrates his first goal for Celtic, in the Scottish Cup against Morton

Darren Jackson makes it 2–0 and Celtic are going through to the next round

Brattbakk – finished off an intricate move which also involved Burley and Larsson. Celtic could even afford the luxury of a second missed penalty in as many games – this time Larsson was the culprit, firing his shot against the crossbar.

A trip to Tannadice to face Dundee United is not the most welcoming prospect at the best of times. On a bitterly cold Tuesday in January it's the sort of game you might like to avoid altogether. The fixture had already been postponed twice because of weather but now it was going ahead. As well as their poor recent run of away form, Celtic had other problems with team selection. Tom Boyd was unavailable through suspension, while Alan Stubbs was injured which meant a recall to defensive duty for Rico Annoni and David Hannah, who would be facing his old club.

Wim Jansen had already highlighted the problems faced by Celtic in many away games when the opposition tried to muscle their way through the match. No one could ever accuse Dundee United of taking a physical approach to a game and this, bizarrely, could work to Celtic's favour. For once, away from home, they could play something approaching their natural game. Celtic started well, playing with as much poise and flair as anyone could muster under the conditions. They looked much the better side for the first 20 minutes but then, incredibly, found themselves a goal behind with United's first attack of the game. With Annoni outnumbered at the back, Pedersen and Zetterlund managed to work the ball to Kjell Olofsson who had a clear shot and took full advantage.

Celtic were stunned, but continued to press forward without any success and went in

The game against Morton marked yet another clean sheet for Celtic keeper Jonathan Gould

at half-time a goal down. This was an ominous prospect for the Celtic support. With the exception of the 3–2 game against Motherwell at Fir Park in September, Celtic had never successfully come back from being a goal behind. Their hardy contingent of travelling fans feared the worst when the Celtic challenge began to fade early in the second half. United began to take control of the game, knocking the ball around with ease and denying Celtic space and opportunity. Once again, on the hour mark, Jackson came on for Brattbakk and once again the supporters had cause to be grateful. It was Jackson who set up Lambert in the seventy-seventh minute. The midfielder's fierce shot was initially saved by Dykstra but he could only get one hand on it. The ball looked as if it might yet go for a corner but Donnelly, following up, was sharp enough to take the rebound and send it into the net from a tight angle.

Celtic were level, but were still not playing at their best. Despite their continued pressure it looked as if another disappointment was on the cards, especially with Gould being pressed into action to deal with a renewed burst of attacking from the home side. But, with two minutes left and another draw looming, Celtic found that luck was on their side. Long-throw expert Rico Annoni sent a looping throw-in down the right flank and into the path of Larsson who then flicked it on to Donnelly. The young forward cut the ball back to the oncoming Burley who let loose with a fierce drive. Whether the ball would have gone into the net on its own is a question for the ages, but the fact is that, as Skoldmark lunged to try to block it, the shot clipped his heel and went looping into a shallow chip which took it over Dykstra's diving body and into the net.

Celtic had come to Dundee, they had battled hard, they had played poorly, but, most importantly, they had the points.

Celtic 2   Dundee United 1
Donnelly   Olofsson
Burley

Celtic: Gould, Annoni, Hannah, Rieper, Mahé, McNamara, Burley, Lambert, Wieghorst, Brattbakk, Larsson

Substitutes: Donnelly for McNamara, Jackson for Brattbakk

Bookings: McNamara, Hannah, Lambert

Attendance: 14,004

THE PRESSURE MOUNTS

Aberdeen v Celtic
2 February 1998

The race for the 1997–98 Premier Division title was the tightest anyone could remember. For the past two seasons it had become a two-horse race between Rangers and Celtic and cynics might point out that's one more horse than usual – given Rangers' dominance of the division for the past nine years. Now a third horse had entered the race in the shape of a determined challenge from Jim Jefferies' Hearts side. But, although the league was competitive, the competition was caused as much by dropped points as anything else. No one was dominating the division. Celtic had lost silly points at Fir Park and McDiarmid Park, Rangers had lost at Dunfermline and even Hearts had gone through that spell at Christmas when they had picked up only two points against Dundee United, Celtic, Rangers and Hibs. Yet, despite all these dropped points, you could scarcely slip a cigarette paper between them.

The last weekend in January saw another crack appear in the Ibrox defence of their title when Rangers were surprisingly beaten 2–0 by St Johnstone. Hearts had won their game against Dundee United quite comfortably, while Celtic had a Saturday off. Because Celtic's home game against Aberdeen was being televised it meant that they would not be playing until Monday night. It also meant that, taking the weekend results into consideration, they would go joint top with Hearts and Rangers if they could beat the Dons. Indeed, if they could beat them by six goals Celtic would be top on goal difference. That was an unrealistic proposition and it became apparent that the three points would be enough, goal difference could sort itself out later on.

Celtic were again without Tom Boyd through suspension and Craig Burley took the captain's armband as he had at Tannadice against Dundee United. Other than that Wim Jansen had no worries and he was able to field the team which, with Regi Blinker left out because of his recent poor form, was becoming recognised as his most effective combination. With all of his attacking options open to him he again went for Brattbakk, who had yet to score in the league, and left Jackson and Donnelly on the bench.

Aberdeen had had a fairly miserable season so far and were still flirting with the relegation zone as they lay second bottom, only a point above Hibs. This was an entirely unsatisfactory position for a club with a proud history, and they came to Celtic Park looking for at least a measure of retribution for two comprehensive defeats early in the season. Certainly they started as if they meant business and seemed determined to carry the game to Celtic. Before the huge television audience had settled in its seat, Aberdeen had almost taken the lead. Almost straight from the kick-off Eoin Jess and Stephen Glass linked up to create an opening for Mike Newell, which the former English Premiership striker squandered when it would have been easier to score. Moments later, Jess himself conjured up an opportunity which required Jonathan Gould to be on top form to deal with. With only five minutes gone Aberdeen could have been two ahead with Celtic still not really in the game. Three minutes later they scored the goal they had been threatening, to leave the home crowd shocked rather than surprised. There was an element of luck about it – David Rowson's shot was deflected past Gould by Paul Lambert – but since Celtic had grabbed the points at Tannadice in exactly the same way they could hardly complain about a little karmic comeback.

Celtic were a goal down but there was no panic. The lessons which Jansen had been instilling into them all season were starting to take effect. It was early, there were 82 minutes left, and there was no need to chase the game. There was enough self-belief in this Celtic side to realise that if they played their own game the results would come. That's exactly what they did, although they were now playing with a little more focus and urgency. Celtic continued to pass the ball, to make space and to put Aberdeen under pressure. Despite losing that opening goal, the Celtic defence was holding firm and solid enough for Stubbs to come up for a McNamara corner. As the ball was delivered into the box Stubbs put in a good header which crashed against the bar and served notice that Celtic were getting back into the game. A short time later the Aberdeen woodwork took another hammering, this time from a Jackie McNamara snap-shot.

As Celtic continued to press, Aberdeen were beginning to show signs of creaking under the strain. It was not a question of if Celtic would equalise, rather it was a question of when. The answer was 21 minutes, when Morten Wieghorst added another to his tally for the season. This time the ball had been flicked on by the head of Alan Stubbs and Wieghorst, who was rapidly proving to be deadly in front of goal, smacked it past Leighton. It was the Dane's sixth goal of what was turning out to be the best season of his career. That equaliser simply broke down the flood gates as far as Celtic were concerned. Aberdeen continued to resist, but it was token rather than dogged. Within another quarter of an hour Celtic had their noses in front and the game was over as a contest. The second goal came in 35 minutes as a result of an aerial ballet between two of Celtic's Scandinavian contingent. Stubbs launched another of his precision free-kicks into the box, Rieper reached it with his head and nodded it on to Larsson who, in turn, headed it past Leighton.

Aberdeen were entitled to wonder what had gone wrong. They had come to Glasgow determined to make a game of it, they had gone a goal in front and now, with the half-time whistle about to blow, the match seemed well beyond them. Certainly as they went down the tunnel at half-time Aberdeen looked like beaten men. When they came out for the restart there was none of the spark that there had been in the first half. Celtic quickly got back into the groove with a McNamara header going wide and Leighton having to save from a Burley header in the opening minutes. Celtic continued to dominate and the only surprise was that it took them so long to add to their total. Leighton, to his credit, had been performing heroics and one such save had denied Darren Jackson – on for Brattbakk after an hour, naturally. From the resulting corner McNamara sent a long cross to the back post which found Donnelly with space and time. Although he had scored from such a position before, this time Donnelly had the presence of mind to chip the ball back into the area. Rieper was favourite to reach it until Leighton made a great diving save to tip the ball off the defender's head. Tragically for Leighton and Aberdeen he only succeeded in tipping it as far as Jackson who hammered it home, despite a ruck of red shirts on the goal line.

It was 3–1 and the game was over. The lessons of Tannadice a fortnight previously had been learned and once again Celtic had shown the mental fortitude to come back from behind to win the game. Now, with all three teams level on points at the top of the table and Celtic facing Hearts at Tynecastle this weekend, surely something had to give.

Celtic 3   Aberdeen 1
Wieghorst   Rowson
Larsson
Jackson

Celtic: Gould, Annoni, Stubbs, Rieper, Mahé, McNamara, Burley, Lambert, Wieghorst, Larsson, Brattbakk

Substitutes: Jackson for Brattbakk, Donnelly for Larsson

Bookings: None

Attendance: 46,608

A MISSED OPPORTUNITY

Hearts v Celtic
8 February 1998

The three contenders at the top of the Scottish Premier Division went into the weekend of 7 February knowing that by the end of the 48-hour period the situation should be a lot clearer. At three o'clock on the Saturday they would start all square but by tea-time on Sunday – the Hearts v Celtic game was being televised – there should be some daylight between them. That theory gained even more credence when the inconsistency which had bedevilled all three teams struck again. Fans were stunned when on the Saturday, Rangers could only manage a 1–1 draw against Dunfermline. Celtic knew that if they beat Hearts at Tynecastle the following day they would then open up a two-point gap on Rangers and put themselves three points in front of Hearts.

Celtic had already beaten Hearts twice this season by greater margins than the 2–1 and 1–0 scorelines might suggest. But Hearts were showing a great deal of determination and mental toughness as the season progressed. Jim Jefferies was proving himself to be a shrewd and skilful manager and had been able to blend a side which mixed youth with Continental experience and was brimful of confidence. For all that, Hearts had been a little backward at coming forward in the first two encounters. They seemed to be prepared to sit in and allow Celtic to come at them, and they had paid the price on both occasions. Their fans must have been encouraged then when they started the game with a Colin Cameron shot which Jonathan Gould had to be at full stretch to tip away. Unfortunately for the Tynecastle supporters, this was just about their team's only contribution to the first half.

Jansen had gone for a 3-5-2 formation and, with the extra midfielder strengthening the attack, Celtic simply swept forward. Cameron's shot was a momentary glitch as the Celtic machine got itself into top gear.

Hearts were fielding substitute keeper Roddy McKenzie in place of Gilles Rousset and the youngster almost gave away the opening goal in eight minutes. McKenzie took the cross from McNamara but then dropped the ball at the feet of Brattbakk who pounced, only to see Dave McPherson clear it off the line. This was a strong indication of things to come for both Brattbakk and Celtic.

If Celtic needed any further hint that things were not going to go their way it came only four minutes later when Morten Wieghorst had the ball in the net, only for referee Tait to disallow it for the use of a hand in what seemed to be a dubious decision. Despite this, it seemed like only a temporary respite for Hearts and a momentary delay for Celtic in opening the score. Even at this stage it was plain that the Celtic tactics were working. Celtic were attacking Hearts on the flanks and as McNamara and Mahé made their runs down right and left, the defence was stretched wider and wider allowing Larsson and Brattbakk space for their runs. Celtic continued to press and again almost took the lead in the twenty-third minute when Lambert found Stubbs in space at the edge of the box. The tall defender hit an immaculately struck shot which seemed to be perfectly placed. McKenzie was well beaten but the ball smacked off the foot of the post and out into play again. Larsson had also come close on two occasions; the first time his shot was well held by McKenzie and on the second McKenzie beat him to the ball as the Swede raced on to a pass from Brattbakk.

Hearts were merely hanging on at this stage. There was the occasional attacking flurry, but this was very much a rearguard action. The fighting retreat came unstuck in 42 minutes when Celtic finally took the lead. Although Brattbakk had yet to score, his direct running frequently caused problems for defences. This time he ran into the box with the ball at his feet and slipped a delicate pass to Larsson, who was inside him on his right. As Larsson steadied himself for his shot he was tackled by Paul Ritchie in what seemed to be a clear penalty. Larsson was busy claiming for the penalty as he tumbled to the ground but, at the same time, the ball broke to McNamara who showed commendable composure in hitting it cleanly into the net. McNamara had been Celtic's best player in the first half and it was appropriate that he should score. The timing of the goal, just three minutes before half-time, was psychologically important, since Hearts were probably thinking they had weathered the storm.

The second half saw the Hearts goal under siege, as it had been in the first. There was simply no respite for the maroon-shirted defenders as Celtic continued to press forward in search of a second goal to kill off the game. But, despite almost unrelenting pressure, Celtic simply could not score. Brattbakk was the worst offender and missed several chances to open his league account. One miss, in 57 minutes, was particularly hard to swallow in the light of subsequent events. Larsson had shot from close range and McKenzie had done well to get to it but he could only parry it away. Brattbakk, sliding in to take the rebound, contrived to put the ball over the bar from less than six yards out. It was a golden opportunity to settle the game and take the points and it was a miss which Celtic would come to rue.

At the time, however, they simply carried on attacking. In the second half it seemed like the Celtic players were queuing up to have a crack at the Hearts goal. Rieper headed wide; Larsson had a shot saved; Burley just skimmed the crossbar; McKenzie saved at the feet of Brattbakk; even Stephane Mahé had a shot tipped on to the bar. This was simply a shooting gallery, but still the Hearts defence held firm and carried its luck. Brattbakk did have the ball in the net in 82 minutes but was ruled offside. Shortly after that he was replaced by Jackson.

Even though they had not been able to score a second goal, Celtic still appeared to have this game well won. McKenzie's marvellous save from Mahé in 87 minutes seemed to be the last throw of the dice and Celtic were content to defend. Although they had been attacking with vigour, they were not defending with their customary venom. Once again they were sitting a little too deep in the final third of the field and allowing Hearts a lot of space in front of them. Hearts rallied a little with Hamilton having a shot well saved by Gould and having an overhead effort from a Ritchie free-kick go just wide.

Celtic fans had seen this all before and those with longer memories were starting to get a bad feeling. The sensible thing to do would have been to give the ball to Jackson or McNamara and have them take it for a walk down to the Hearts corner flag. But with Celtic still not clearing the ball and referee Tait adding on an unconscionable amount of injury time Hearts finally took their chance.

Hearts had brought on José Quitongo midway through the second half but the rubber-legged winger hadn't shown much. Then, with the game 94-minutes old, he had a shot on goal which appeared to rebound safely off the Celtic defence. The ball fell to McCann who also tried a shot, this time rebounding off Annoni. The ball came back to Quitongo who wriggled through the Celtic defence before firing a shot which Gould appeared to have covered, until it came off Mahé's arm and was deflected past him into the net. The Hearts bench was delirious, Jim Jefferies staged a one-man pitch invasion and Tynecastle was in uproar. It was an appalling goal for Celtic to lose – there were six Celtic defenders around Quitongo at the time – and the stricken looks on their faces said it all.

Hearts had got out of jail, Celtic had blown what should have been a safe three points, and we were back where we started with all three teams still level on points.

Celtic 1   Hearts 1
McNamara   Quitongo

Celtic: Gould, Annoni, Stubbs, Rieper, McNamara, Burley, Lambert, Wieghorst, Mahé, Larsson, Brattbakk

Substitutes: Jackson for Brattbakk

Bookings: Annoni, Burley, Lambert

Attendance: 17,657

HARALD TO THE FOUR

Kilmarnock v Celtic
21 February 1998

With 12 games left in the league programme and all three top teams level on points, the run-in was going to be a question of nerve. Whichever team had the mental toughness to survive the next dozen games would be the league champions, it was as simple as that. But before the league battle could be joined, there was still the question of the Scottish Cup. All three sides were still involved and they could have a weekend free from worrying about the league while they got on with their Cup duties.

The fourth round of the Scottish Cup saw Celtic paired with Dunfermline at East End Park, in a game which would take place on a Monday night to accommodate the requirements of television. This was the fifth meeting between the two sides this season but if they were getting sick of the sight of each other there was no sign of it. For Celtic, Tom Boyd was available for selection again. He had served his three-game league suspension and the Cup match would help get him back to match sharpness for the run-in. Rico Annoni dropped back to the subs bench and Jansen fielded an otherwise predictable 4-4-2 formation.

The two teams knew each other well enough by now, and Dunfermline were out to prove that the Cup is a great leveller. They more than held their own in a scrappy first half – even forcing a great save out of Jonathan Gould from Andy Tod just on the half-hour mark. At the other end his opposite number Ian Westwater had pulled off an equally good save to deny Harald Brattbakk. The sides went in at the interval still goalless, but with Morten Wieghorst cursing his luck. For the second match in succession the Dane had scored what appeared to be a decent goal only to see it chalked off. This time Wieghorst had hammered home a cross from Mahé only for it to be ruled offside. To complete his misery, Wieghorst was booked for complaining about the decision.

Mahé was having perhaps his best game in a Celtic jersey and it was he who scored the opening goal five minutes into the second half. Mahé had made one of his increasingly frequent runs down the left-hand channel, but he wasn't getting a great deal of change from Den Bieman. Still retaining possession, the Frenchman checked inside, looked up and fired a blistering shot into the net. The goal put Celtic in the driving seat and in 67 minutes they added a second. Larsson sent the ball out to McNamara on the right and the winger began a run into the area before sending a beautifully judged ball into the path of Harald Brattbakk. A grateful Brattbakk had only to check his stride slightly and sidefoot the ball into the net. Ten minutes from time Dunfermline looked like pulling themselves back into the game when a French cross found David Bingham at the near post and left him with a simple job to score. Although the score was now 2–1, Celtic remained calm and ran the clock down retaining possession comfortably until the end of the game.

With their passage to the quarter-final of the Cup safely navigated, Celtic could turn their attention back to the league. With all three sides on 49 points, goal difference could play a big part. Rangers had a goal difference of +29, Celtic were second with +26, while Hearts were the weakest of the three on +21. Rangers' superior goal difference was founded on the free-scoring exploits of Marco Negri in the early part of the season but the Italian had lost his touch after Christmas and the goals were drying up. Celtic, for their part, knew that they would have to win games, but also win them well, to make up the three-goal deficit on Rangers.

When Celtic came out to face Kilmarnock at Celtic Park on Saturday, 21 February, they were greeted with a louder than normal roar. The club had completed the new south-west corner of the ground which allowed an additional 2,650 fans to see the team. There was also an appreciative cheer for former Celt Gordon Marshall who was making his first visit to Celtic Park since his transfer to Killie. Kilmarnock had yet to score a goal against Celtic this season and they were also suffering the effects of a Cup defeat the previous week by local rivals Ayr United. Celtic's defence might have expected an easy time of it, with the onus being thrown on their forwards to score and score often.

Certainly it looked like Celtic were determined to get things off to an appropriate start when, with only four minutes on the clock, Larsson sent Brattbakk through, but the Norwegian was denied by Marshall's courageous dive at his feet. Marshall's heroics had merely delayed the opening goal which finally came in 11 minutes. Larsson picked up a ball from McNamara and sent it across to the left, where Brattbakk's beautifully

Stephane Mahe celebrates in typically Gallic fashion after scoring in the 2–1 Scottish Cup win against Dunfermline

judged run left him to side-foot the ball home while the Kilmarnock defence claimed unsuccessfully for offside. It was his first league goal for Celtic and he will score few more easily. Seven minutes later he should have made it two when he picked up another ball from Larsson, dribbled round Marshall and then fired a shot which trundled agonisingly to the line before hitting the post. Again, it was merely a delay and the second came in 37 minutes when Celtic took one of their trademark free-kicks and Burley slid the ball into the area for Brattbakk to stroke home.

Celtic were well in control of the match by now and in the second half, with the home team pressing for more goals, Marshall was all that stood between Kilmarnock and a rout. He saved again in a one-on-one situation with Brattbakk and forced the attacker to shoot against the post in another attack, this time the ball rolling along the goal line without actually going in. But not even Marshall could stop Brattbakk for long. The hat-trick came in the seventieth minute, when Brattbakk once again fired home from close range after Simon Donnelly had provided the telling pass.

Brattbakk had scored three and could have had as many more. What was more significant was that he seemed to be shaping up as the kind of striker Celtic had desperately needed. All of these goals were snapped up in the penalty box from the sort of chances which had previously gone a-begging. With only three minutes left Brattbakk scored the pick of the bunch for his fourth. Burley found Jackson, who had again come on as a substitute, this time for Larsson, who neatly cut the ball inside for Brattbakk. As the Norwegian got past a defender and bore down on goal, Marshall came out to narrow the angle, but this time Brattbakk anticipated the dive and timed his shot perfectly, sliding the ball under his body.

It was a personal triumph for the Norwegian who had answered many of his critics with this performance.

'It is tremendous to score four in one game, but it is always more important that the team wins,' he said selflessly. 'I have had lots of letters of support from fans who said they knew I was a good player who would do it and I always believed that.'

While Celtic were beating Kilmarnock 4–0, Rangers and Hearts were also winning. Rangers' 2–1 win over Hibs meant that Celtic had now eaten up the three-goal deficit in goal difference. They were both now on +30 and Rangers remained top only by virtue of having scored more goals.

Celtic 4   Kilmarnock 0
Brattbakk (4)

Celtic: Gould, Boyd, Rieper, Stubbs, Mahé, McNamara, Lambert, Burley, Wieghorst, Brattbakk, Larsson

Substitutes: Donnelly for McNamara, Annoni for Rieper, Jackson for Larsson

Bookings: None

Attendance: 49,231

Right: Brattbakk discovered a goalden touch with a one-man demolition job against Kilmarnock at Celtic Park

Below: Brattbakk scores the third of his four, spoiling ex-Celtic keeper Gordon Marshall's return to his old ground

HARALD STRIKES AGAIN

Dunfermline v Celtic
25 February 1998

The win against Kilmarnock had been gained in considerable style but at a heavy cost. The Celtic injury list was mounting at a time when the team was under a lot of pressure from fixtures. After the Kilmarnock game, physio Brian Scott's treatment room must have resembled an army field hospital. Jackie McNamara had picked up an ankle knock and aggravated a knee injury, Alan Stubbs took a thigh knock in the same game, Paul Lambert had a bruised calf and Marc Rieper, who had been sent home in the week before the Killie match with a stomach bug, had complained of feeling unwell during the match. On top of this Regi Blinker, who had been left out of the squad since the St Johnstone game because of poor form, had picked up a calf injury in training. All of this came in addition to an injury list which had already included Rico Annoni and Darren Jackson.

Looking on the brighter side, the forgotten man of Celtic Park was ready for a comeback. Tommy Johnson had played only once, in the opening match against Hibs, and despite missing most of the rest of the season with a double hernia, he was pragmatic enough to know that he no longer fitted in Wim Jansen's plans. From Jansen's point of view that seems a somewhat harsh judgement given Johnson's lack of match practice. However, Johnson was now fit again and hoping to play himself into some kind of form so that he could get a transfer during the summer. Such was the depth of the Celtic injury list and the fragility of the first-team squad that Johnson found himself named in the 14 to play Dunfermline in this midweek fixture. In the end Rieper and Lambert made the game but without Stubbs and McNamara – two of their most influential players in recent weeks – this was very definitely an understrength Celtic side. The absence of

Annoni and Jackson also limited Jansen's tactical options in his substitutions.

They did, however, go into the game boosted with the knowledge that Rangers had dropped points the night before against Kilmarnock. Given their superior goal difference over Hearts, any kind of a win at all against Dunfermline would put Celtic ahead of the Edinburgh side on goal difference and two points clear of Rangers. To win under the circumstances was vital for Celtic, but no one could have predicted just how they would win.

David Hannah filled in for Alan Stubbs, Simon Donnelly took McNamara's midfield role and this understrength side simply tore Dunfermline apart, emphasising their credentials in the championship race. This was a huge psychological victory, not only in winning but in winning in such style. The capacity crowd was, perhaps, beginning to feel that they were seeing the future champions in action. Dunfermline had been doughty competitors in both League and Cup and, notwithstanding the Pars' early victory, there was never much in it when the two sides had met previously. Not tonight. This game ended as a contest in just under four minutes with a moment of magic between Donnelly and Larsson. Donnelly, with his back to the goal, had sent a clever flick into the Dunfermline penalty box. There were several defenders between Larsson and the ball, but somehow he wriggled through them to slide home his shot with pin-point accuracy.

Larsson was once again the puppet-master for this Celtic side as he pulled the strings to create one of their best displays of the season. No one was happier than Harald Brattbakk, who continued his scoring form of the weekend with another brace in the first half here. His first goal was a magnificent 25-yarder which rocketed into the top corner; his second came as a result of another piece of genius from Larsson and a perfectly weighted pass which left the Norwegian with only Westwater to beat. There had been those who questioned Brattbakk's form when he had scored only one goal in nine appearances. Ten days and three games later his record read: played 12, scored 8.

With goal difference so vital, there was no let-up in the Celtic pressure. They came at the Dunfermline defence again and again. Manager Bert Paton later criticised his team, pointing out that for all

Dunfermline's Andy Smith kept a tight hold on Brattbakk but the
Viking raider still scored a couple in Celtic's 5–1 win

the good they had done they might as well have been on the terracings.
That was harsh because there weren't many teams who could live with
Celtic in this kind of form, and they had to be doing something right to
have kept it down to three at half-time.

The second half saw more of the same from Celtic, as well as the
introduction of a couple of almost forgotten faces. Phil O'Donnell
hadn't played since October, but he came on for Burley in the sixty-
fourth minute and scored within seconds. O'Donnell joined the Celtic
forwards in the box for a corner and when Hannah flicked on
Donnelly's cross, O'Donnell was there to head it home for a welcome
return. Four minutes later Morten Wieghorst celebrated his twenty-

seventh birthday in some style with a piece of ball-juggling followed by a looping shot which crashed into the net past Westwater to make it five.

Dunfermline managed a consolation goal in the seventy-second minute with an Andy Tod header from a Greg Shields cross. One of the biggest cheers of the night was reserved for the reintroduction of Tommy Johnson when the chirpy Geordie came on, also in the seventy-second minute. Tragically, Johnson never really got the chance to impress and misery was heaped upon misery when he was stretchered off after 13 minutes with damaged knee ligaments following an awkward fall. There wasn't a fan in the ground who didn't feel for Johnson as he was carried round the running track and into the dressing-room.

Tommy Johnson's comeback against Dunfermline lasts 13 minutes before he is stretchered off with another injury. Celtic went on to win 5–1

Tommy Johnson's personal nightmare apart, this was a great night's work for Celtic. They were top of the league and unbeaten since 27 December. Despite their injury problems they were growing in stature and confidence with every game and looked like having what it took for the run-in.

After the match Wim Jansen acknowledged what every fan knew.

'It's nice to be top,' he said, 'but the most important thing is to stay there. It's impossible to say whether we will win the Championship, you just never know what is going to happen in this game.'

Jansen normally played the press with a straight bat but even he could not hide his pleasure with his team after this game. He allowed himself a small joke at the expense of one-touch wonder Phil O'Donnell.

'I've told Phil it's okay to score with his second touch next time,' said the Dutchman wryly.

Celtic 5	Dunfermline 1
Larsson	Tod
Brattbakk (2)	
O'Donnell	
Wiehgorst	

Celtic: Gould, Boyd, Mahé, Rieper, Hannah, Larsson, Burley, Brattbakk, Lambert, Wieghorst

Substitutes: O'Donnell for Burley, Johnson for Larsson, Mackay for Johnson

Bookings: None

Attendance: 48,502

DAYLIGHT

Hibs v Celtic
28 February 1998

The last Saturday in February was another of those make-or-break days which would play such a vital part in deciding who would hoist the league flag at the start of the following season. Celtic travelled to Edinburgh to face Hibs, at the end of a week in which they had scored nine goals, conceded only one and gone to the top of the league. Meanwhile in Glasgow, Rangers were hosts to Hearts. Unlike Celtic, Rangers went into the game with the surprise draw against Kilmarnock haunting them. Hearts, who were level on points with Celtic but trailing on goal difference, went into the match with the burden of not yet having beaten either of the Old Firm in five previous encounters this season.

With no disrespect to Kilmarnock or Dunfermline, Celtic could face a much stiffer test at Easter Road than they had against either of those sides. Hibs were lodged firmly at the bottom of the table five points adrift of Motherwell, but they had recently been able to persuade Motherwell boss Alex McLeish to move from Fir Park to Easter Road. Motherwell's side under McLeish's stewardship had already split the honours with Celtic this season – their three games had ended in a win to each team with the other game drawn. McLeish's Motherwell had also been instrumental in twice bringing Celtic down to earth with a bump when they were flying high. So the Celtic Park men would have been in no doubt that McLeish would encourage his new side to dig deep and find their combative qualities in the relegation dogfight.

Wim Jansen had a fair idea what to expect and, once again, he hoped to adopt a 3-5-2 formation to give his team the edge with the extra man in midfield. But an eleventh-hour drama almost scuppered his plans.

Craig Burley had been taken off midway through the second half against Dunfermline and he had been suffering from recurring back and calf problems. He hadn't trained between the two games and only made the decision to declare himself fit minutes before the game. The injury would plague Burley for the rest of the season but the gritty midfielder was determined that nothing would stand between him and a Championship medal.

After the injury problems in the game against St Johnstone both McNamara and Stubbs were back and, with Burley ready to play, the Celtic team took on a familiar look. The performance had a horribly familiar look too as nerves appeared to get the better of some of the players on occasion. There was an edginess and an uncertainty about some aspects of their play. Fortunately, the extra man in midfield gave them the advantage and the trio of Lambert, Burley and Wieghorst controlled the middle of the park quite comfortably.

It was Hibs who shaped up best in the first few minutes of the game. With the game barely 60 seconds old, Grant Brebner, who was on loan from Manchester United, got on the end of a poorly cleared free-kick and chipped the ball over Gould. As the Easter Road crowd rose in expectation of a shock goal the ball hit the crossbar. Ten minutes later Gould was in action again when Barry Lavety quickly turned and shot, but the Celtic keeper held it comfortably. Despite these early forays, the game was developing largely as expected with the home side doing their best to stifle the match. It was unreasonable for them to expect the sort of result they had got on the opening day of the season but, perhaps, if they got enough men behind the ball and hung on grimly enough, they might manage a precious point.

The Hibs game plan came unstuck in 25 minutes when Celtic took the lead with a scrappy goal which was a pretty fair reflection of the game. McNamara's corner out on the left found Larsson who flicked it on with his head. Stubbs and the Hibs keeper Bryan Gunn went up together and the keeper looked favourite but, under pressure from the Celtic defender, he dropped it. The ball fell onto the goal line and fortunately for Hibs there were no Celtic players close enough to take advantage. A rushed clearance from Jean-Marc Boco, however, landed at the feet of Marc Rieper who had come up in support of the

THE GLORY, GLORY BHOYS

forwards. The big defender did everything that was required, getting his weight over the ball, keeping it down and firing it into the net from close to the penalty spot. The Hibs players and fans were incensed, they howled that Stubbs had fouled Gunn when he was challenging for the ball. Referee Jim McCluskey waved away their protests and allowed the goal to stand in a courageous decision – which was later proved correct by television replays. Celtic went in a goal ahead at half-time and knew that it could have been two had a Burley effort five minutes after Rieper's goal not grazed the crossbar and gone over.

Hibs started the second half with a hiss and a roar and the Celtic defence had to be on their mettle as the home side came close to an equaliser on several occasions. Former Celt John Hughes sent a header over the bar from a Harper free-kick, then Lavety got into the act with a couple of good efforts. The first, a shot, was blocked on the goal line by Alan Stubbs. The second, a header this time, was held by Gould on his line. And, as Hibs began to look a beaten side, Celtic almost put the game beyond doubt with an audacious effort from Stephane Mahé. The Frenchman fired what appeared to be a long-range clearance from inside his own half. But, after travelling the best part of 60 yards, the ball began to dip – reminiscent of Pele's great effort in the 1970 World Cup – and a frantic Bryan Gunn had to scramble back to just tip it over the bar.

But with the game almost finished and nothing much happening on the field, the biggest roar of the day erupted from the Celtic supporters in the South and West stands. Hearts had been winning 2–1 at Ibrox, which would effectively have left the Ibrox side trailing five points behind both Celtic and Hearts. But with almost the last kick of the game Rangers midfielder Jorg Albertz had equalised to make it 2–2. Rangers and Hearts had both dropped points and Celtic were two points clear at the top of the league. A lot of the Celtic fans in the crowd questioned the cheering of a Rangers goal even as they were celebrating but, on this occasion, the end justified the means. The German midfielder had put Celtic on top of the league.

This was a very big win for Celtic, much bigger than the 1–0 scoreline might suggest. It was the sort of fixture in which they could

Another Manager of the Month award for Jansen – his third in just seven months

not even entertain dropping a point if they had serious pretensions to the title. In the end they did exactly what they had to do. It wasn't always attractive but it got the job done. It may not have been achieved in the cavalier manner of the Celtic tradition but the fans were beginning to realise that trading points for flair was not necessarily such a raw deal.

'People always said the fans would never accept a Celtic team who didn't constantly play attacking football,' said Alan Stubbs after the match. 'But I think we've shown by already winning a trophy playing attractive, intelligent football that it can be the right way.'

Three quarters of the season had been completed. There were only nine games to go and finally Celtic could see some daylight between them and the rest of the division.

All they had to do was hold their nerve.

Celtic 1   Hibs 0
Rieper

Celtic: Gould, Boyd, Stubbs, Rieper, McNamara, Lambert, Burley, Wieghorst, Mahé, Brattbakk, Larsson

Substitutes: Donnelly for Brattbakk, O'Donnell for McNamara

Bookings: None

Attendance: 15,137

A COSTLY SLIP

Dundee United v Celtic
15 March 1998

These were heady times to be a Celtic fan. Never mind the nip and tuck of the title race, there was still the Scottish Cup to be dealt with and with the Coca-Cola Cup already in the trophy cabinet the notion of the elusive Treble flirted seductively with the imagination. But for that to happen, Celtic would have to face Dundee United, not once, but twice. In one of those double-headers which characterised the Coca-Cola Cup, Celtic and United would play each other twice in a week – once in the Scottish Cup, once in the league.

Although they were heady times for the fans, they were tiring times for the players. Some of the Celtic squad, Harald Brattbakk for instance, had not had a proper close-season break and were effectively playing two seasons back to back. Being involved in all three competitions for the first time in 15 years was wonderful if you were on the terraces, but enervating if you were in the dressing-room. A few weeks previously, after the comprehensive win at Kilmarnock, Jansen had hinted that he might buy new faces for the league run-in. Whether he had been thinking aloud or whether he could not find anyone suitable we will probably never know, but the fact was that he was going to have to finish the season with a squad which was starting to succumb to the rigours imposed by their own success.

The latest casualty was Jackie McNamara who would miss both Dundee United games after injuring his ankle against Hibs. This was seen as something of a mixed blessing since McNamara was also suffering from a niggling knee injury which could also do with a rest. United too had their personnel problems for the Cup tie. Kjell Olofsson had undergone cartilage surgery just ten days before this game, but insisted he was fit to play. Erik Pedersen also insisted that he could

Brattbakk opens the scoring for Celtic in the 3–2 game against Dundee United

handle the game, despite having been up all night – his wife had given birth to their son.

Despite recent setbacks, Celtic have an impressive record in the Scottish Cup and it had been 12 years since they had lost a quarter-final. With 11 minutes gone they looked like keeping that record intact – thanks to Harald Brattbakk who was rapidly emerging as a Cup specialist. One of Brattbakk's great skills is playing on the shoulder of the last man and when Larsson spotted him starting his run he put the ball directly into his path. The United defenders appealed in vain for off-side, while Brattbakk took his time in controlling the ball and rounding Dykstra before scoring the first goal. United, however, were not lying down this time and within seven minutes the scores were level with a goal which seemed to have been conjured out of nowhere. Robbie Winters sent a long speculative ball into the Celtic box which eluded the head of Marc Rieper and fell kindly for Kjell Olofsson who

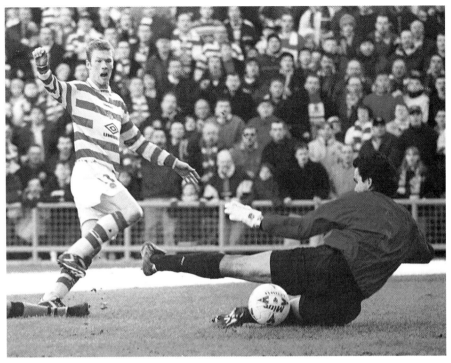

*Tannadice keeper Sieb Dykstra must have been sick of the sight of
Celtic attackers; Wieghorst scores the second*

was able to strike it high into the net. Gould managed to get to the shot
but could only help it in off the post. The goal was greeted with
jubilation by United manager Tommy McLean, who was a little too
vocal in his celebrations, especially those directed at referee Kenny
Clark who McLean felt should have disallowed Celtic's goal. Mr Clark
was less than impressed with McLean's comments and ordered him off.

This was a game which was rapidly turning into a good old-
fashioned Cup tie. It was end-to-end stuff with great saves, near misses
and defensive lapses at both ends. In the second half though, most of
the defensive lapses were happening around Jonathan Gould's goal as
his defenders seemed to lose their composure. In 53 minutes Tom Boyd
slipped making a clearance and could only succeed in sending the ball
to Robbie Winters who turned it to Olofsson. The Swede streaked
towards the Celtic goal, evading defenders before firing a low shot
which beat the advancing Gould with sheer pace. It was United's turn

Relieved Celtic players after an own-goal gives them victory in the Scottish Cup quarter-final against Dundee United

to celebrate but the cheers did not last long. Within three minutes Celtic were level, thanks to Morten Wieghorst who was cleverly spotted by Simon Donnelly after an intricate move involving Brattbakk and Mahé. Dykstra raced off his line but Wieghorst kept his head and calmly nutmegged the despairing Dykstra to put Celtic level.

United were still getting the better of Celtic in the closing stages but Gould was on top form to make two great saves from Olofsson who, with four goals against them, had become something of a thorn in Celtic's flesh. With Gould denying Olofsson, the game seemed headed for a replay – an extra fixture Celtic could well do without – when fate took a hand in the cruellest of manners. Burley took a free-kick deep in his own half in what might well have been Celtic's last throw of the dice. He sent the ball to Brattbakk who ran half the length of the pitch before sending it to Larsson. Spotting that Brattbakk was still running Larsson sent an awkward ball back into the box which the striker just failed to reach. Fortunately for Celtic, Pedersen, who had been tracking back, was right behind Brattbakk to turn the ball into his own net with his knee. It was a cruel blow, more desperately so bearing in mind that it had happened to new dad Pedersen.

Dundee United would have been terribly discouraged by the Cup defeat which, with them in mid-table, effectively ended their season in competitive terms. But the 'return fixture' in the league the following Sunday would give them a chance for revenge. Celtic had beaten them five times out of five this season and Tommy McLean was determined that it would not be six.

By the time the two teams met on that Sunday you could hardly find a Celtic fan who did not believe that the league was all but won. The gap which Celtic had opened in the game against Hibs was threatening to turn into a chasm. The previous day Hearts had drawn at Kilmarnock, while Rangers had lost at Motherwell. A win against Dundee United would put Celtic seven points clear of Rangers and four points clear of Hearts. Three points on home territory would be enough to make it all but certain that the league would be all over bar the shouting, or so the fans reasoned. The fact that there were still eight games to go was neither here nor there.

Wim Jansen fielded an unchanged side for the league fixture but although the personnel were unchanged the tactics were not, and this time Celtic lined up 4-3-3. One concern for the Celtic fans was the current form of Henrik Larsson. The influential Swede had dominated the first half of the season but had only scored twice in 11 games since the turn of the year. Larsson was one of those who were badly in need of a break and he appeared, at least from the terracings, to be a little jaded. But with the Celtic crowd in party mood this Sunday, he was able to turn it on one more time. Larsson was everywhere. His work rate was astonishing as he coaxed, cajoled and prodded his team-mates forward with the ball. Even if he was not scoring himself he was such a threat that his presence inevitably created opportunities for others.

So it was in 27 minutes when Simon Donnelly put Celtic in front. So much attention was being paid to Larsson that the other Celtic attackers were able to profit from it. Wieghorst sent the ball to Brattbakk who flicked it on to Donnelly who struck the ball beautifully with the outside of his boot to send a curling shot past the diving

Dykstra and Larsson battle for the ball as Dundee United dent Celtic's title run-in with a 1–1 draw at Celtic Park

Dykstra. Donnelly's goal was the signal for party time at Celtic Park with the songs and chants coming out full throat as the capacity crowd anticipated a seven-point cushion.

Really this was a game Celtic should have won at a canter. United had very little left in the tank, staring down the barrel of a six-game whitewash. Their only attack of the first half came on the stroke of half-time and Gould made Dolan's weak header look good because he slipped as he went for it. Remarkably, Celtic allowed them back into the match. The defending started too deep, Celtic sat back and gave Dundee United room to play and, eventually, United took the hint. Olofsson – who else – picked up a pass from Easton with all the room in the world. As Lambert made a last, despairing tackle, Celtic's chief tormentor evaded him and cracked home his fifth – and United's fifth too – of the season against Celtic. For the last 15 minutes Celtic found themselves chasing the game and not being able to do anything to get back in front. It was a game they should have won comfortably and in the end they had managed to snatch a draw from the jaws of victory. The atmosphere among the crowd at the end was funereal. What should have been a seven-point lead was now five and there were still games against Rangers and Hearts to come.

Celtic 1   Dundee United 1
Donnelly   Olofsson

Celtic: Gould, Boyd, Stubbs, Rieper, Mahé, Lambert, Burley, Wieghorst, Donnelly, Larsson, Brattbakk

Substitutes: Jackson for Brattbakk, Annoni for Stubbs, O'Donnell for Wieghorst

Bookings: Mahé

Attendance: 48,656

A TEST OF NERVE

Aberdeen v Celtic
21 March 1998

In the early 1980s when Aberdeen and Dundee United, superbly managed by Alex Ferguson and Jim McLean respectively, challenged for domestic and European honours the media dubbed them 'the New Firm'. These were the teams which would challenge the Old Firm of Celtic and Rangers for supremacy in the years to come. The label was misapplied, or perhaps applied a little too early, because in spite of occasional notable successes neither team was able to match the resources of Celtic and Rangers and mount a serious sustained challenge to their supremacy.

It was ironic then that, going into the final quarter of the season, the New Firm of Dundee United and Aberdeen were the only teams who had yet to take a point off Celtic. Every other team in the league had managed at least a draw against Wim Jansen's men. Dundee United had made the most of their last chance by grabbing a draw against the odds at Celtic Park the previous week, and now as Celtic came north to Pittodrie it was Aberdeen who were playing for their pride and to avoid a total whitewash. Certainly the odds favoured Celtic, who had won all three previous fixtures comfortably, but again injuries were stretching the fabric of Jansen's team.

Jackie McNamara's injury had taken a bit longer than expected to clear up, but he was now back training and would be available to start against Aberdeen. However, Alan Stubbs would have to miss the game. The wear and tear of being at the heart of the Celtic defence, along with Marc Rieper, meant the big defender had picked up a groin strain against Dundee United and would miss the match. One man who was bursting to play was Darren Jackson. He had scored his comeback goal against the Dons at Pittodrie, as well as getting another against them at

Celtic Park. Like everyone else in the squad Jackson, who had been sidelined with a hamstring strain, was well aware of the need to put the Dundee United result behind them and get on with defending their five-point advantage.

'We are a good positive side that are great to watch and winning the title is in our own hands,' said Jackson. 'When you go clear at the top you can only lose it, and with our determination and team spirit I'd be very surprised if we did.'

Despite the loss of points against Dundee United it was Celtic's team spirit which had managed to get them through potentially difficult games like Dunfermline and Hibs. That team spirit though would be sorely tested over the remaining weeks of the season, starting with that visit to Pittodrie. When the match began it was Aberdeen who came out like potential champions, with a display that gave the lie to their league position fourth from bottom. Ten points clear of bottom club Hibs, they appeared to have hauled themselves out of danger, but every point was still to be jealously hoarded.

Celtic were, frankly, never at the races in a first half where they scarcely had a shot on target. It was Aberdeen who did the chasing and the harrying and the running of the midfield, while Celtic looked tired and unimaginative. The game was much more physical than anyone expected and referee John Underhill brandished his yellow card six times – an even-handed three for each side. But it was Jonathan Gould who was once again the Celtic hero in the first half. With the outfielders struggling, Celtic's last line of defence showed the sort of form which would ultimately win him a World Cup finals place. With only four minutes on the clock Gould had to be alert to stop a cheeky back-heel from former Celt Brian O'Neil who had latched on to a Jess pass. Ten minutes later Gould, who was threatening to become the busiest Celt on the park, pulled off the pick of his saves from a low, hard drive from Stephen Glass. You would have had difficulty finding anyone who would have taken a bet on Celtic going in level at half-time, and the way the game was going only a man with money to burn would have bet on them being in front.

But, in the sort of development that breaks hearts and wins titles, Celtic got a goal out of nothing. By the forty-fourth minute they had still to have a shot on target but they had managed to win a free-kick on the edge of the Aberdeen area – thanks to a run from Morten Wieghorst. Larsson had scored from a similar situation at Celtic Park earlier in the season but this was a time for pragmatism rather than frivolity. He squared the ball across to Paul Lambert and, with the Dons' defence braced for a shot, Lambert sent a deep cross to the back post into the path of Stephane Mahé. As the Frenchman headed for the by-line to cut it back he was tackled clumsily by David Rowson and brought to the ground.

The Celtic players appealed more in hope than expectation – given that Mr Underhill had refused to penalise heavier tackles in what had been a bruising half. But to the delight of the Celtic contingent and the horror of the home fans the referee pointed to the spot. Burley was now the penalty-taker after Darren Jackson's miss at Motherwell, and he made no mistake. The penalty was Celtic's only shot on target in the first half and, remarkably, despite being under the cosh for so long they went in a goal up.

Aberdeen had been dealt a cruel psychological blow but they came out for the second half still fired up and looking for at least an equaliser and possibly more. Celtic struggled to maintain their advantage and again Jonathan Gould became the man of the hour. One save from the feet of Billy Dodds summed up the mood of an increasingly ill-tempered match. In 57 minutes, Jess made a run down the right and crossed low into the Celtic box. Lambert and Gould got muddled up in trying to clear the ball before Dodds, following up, collided with the keeper on the ground. Gould was incensed and his full and frank opinion of Dodds earned him his first, and only, yellow card of the season. This clash was a signal for a sustained period of Aberdeen attacking in which they won corner after corner but Jonathan Gould and his defenders held firm. If ever the old maxim about strikers winning matches but defenders winning titles was true, this would be it.

With the Celtic defence under pressure Jansen put on Jackson to take some of the strain off his defenders and cause some trouble for Aberdeen. Inevitably, he replaced Brattbakk who had been having a quiet game. Within ten minutes of coming on Jackson almost managed his Aberdeen 'hat-trick'. Celtic won a free-kick out on the left and Larsson bulleted a ball right across the face of the Aberdeen goal. Jackson connected with a superb header which seemed to have the keeper beaten, until Leighton showed his international form by somehow getting his finger tips to the ball and putting it over.

A goal from Jackson then would have sealed the points for Celtic, albeit against the run of play. As it was, thanks to Gould and some resolute defending, the game finished 1–0 and left Celtic still in command at the top of the table. It wasn't pretty but it was one of those nights where the victory was more important than the manner in which it was achieved. Celtic had managed to emulate the traditional hallmark of champions – to win even when they were not playing well.

Celtic 1   Aberdeen 0
Burley

Celtic: Boyd, Mahé, McNamara, Rieper, Annoni, Larsson, Burley, Brattbakk, Lambert, Wieghorst

Substitutes: Jackson for Brattbakk, Donnelly for McNamara, Hannah for Lambert

Bookings: Gould, Mahé, McNamara

Attendance: 18,009

THE PRESSURE BUILDS

Hearts v Celtic
28 March 1998

Normally, Celtic fans like nothing better than starting their Sunday with a mug of tea and a bacon roll, while savouring the account of the previous day's victory. Those who were anticipating reading about a hard-fought game against Aberdeen won under difficult circumstances would have been choking on their roll. The big sports story that Sunday was the suggestion that Wim Jansen might be leaving Celtic Park.

According to the papers, Jansen had a get-out clause in his contract which would allow him to leave at the end of his first year if things did not work out. Conversely, the same clause would allow the club to get rid of him under the same circumstances. The article also suggested that there was a deadline of the end of March for this clause to be activated. The following day Jansen effectively confirmed the story when he went on the club's phone information line and revealed details of his contract. It was no secret that Jansen and Jock Brown did not always see eye to eye, Brown himself admitted as much when these rumours first surfaced earlier in the season. Brown always insisted, however, that he did not have to be someone's best pal to work alongside him. Nonetheless, there was constant media speculation in the days that followed the original story about the relationship between the two men and about Jansen's willingness to leave Celtic Park.

Eventually at the end of a week of rumour and counter-rumour Wim Jansen himself issued a media statement.

'I'm disappointed about the way that information regarding my contract has appeared in the media,' it began. 'I want to make it clear that I have had no part in this and that at no time has the issue been about money. The reason I spoke out last Monday was that I wanted the truth to be known.

'I asked for a clause in my contract that would enable myself and Celtic to review the situation after my first season. I have had some discussions with the club this week and these will continue in the coming weeks. There is no "first of April deadline". I want to assure everyone that I fully intend to be at Celtic until the end of the season. As for the future, I will make a clear decision in due course.

'The most important issue right now is for everyone at Celtic to concentrate on the coming matches. I have nothing further to say on this matter.'

Jock Brown made no public comment, but if Wim Jansen thought his statement would have been the end of things, he was either not as bright as we thought he was or almost impossibly naïve. Instead of settling the argument it merely added fuel to the flames. Although the statement appeared to say not very much at all, you didn't have to look too hard between the lines to see that Jansen wasn't really intending to draw his pension at Celtic. The uncertainty over his future and his unwillingness to confront it over the next few weeks meant the issue would dog Jansen and the club until the end of the season.

While all of this was going on, Jansen also had to concentrate on getting his men ready for one of the biggest games of the season: Hearts were the visitors at Celtic Park and with both sides still locked together on points a win for either of them would go a long way to deciding the outcome of the title race. Although there were injury scares over Paul Lambert and Jackie McNamara, who had both been substituted against Aberdeen, both players had responded to treatment and were able to take their place in Jansen's starting line up. Hearts, for their part, were aware that time was running out for them. It was technically possible to become champions without beating Celtic or Rangers, but it would be hard to claim the title with any credibility under those circumstances. They would have to carry the game to Celtic to make the most of their dwindling opportunities.

In previous encounters Hearts had been cagey; they had played with one man up front at times and been severely punished on at least two occasions for their lack of adventure; on the third occasion they had got out of jail with a late equaliser and they knew it. This time they attacked from the first whistle and the tension in the game could be judged by the fact that referee Bobby Tait booked Marc Rieper for dissent within the opening minute. Hearts were up for this game and Celtic would have to be on their mettle to stop them.

The first Hearts effort from Weir, in three minutes, was countered by a Rieper header two minutes later. The sides seemed to be evenly matched but slowly, and surely, it was Hearts who began to take the upper hand. For once the Celtic midfield failed to perform. Burley was struggling to make every game because of that recurring back injury and while his courage was commendable there was no doubt his mobility was somewhat hampered. His opposite number at Hearts, former Celt Steve Fulton, was getting the better of most of their encounters. Likewise, Cameron had the better of Lambert and Salvatori was man-marking Morten Wieghorst to prevent his forward runs. With the midfield effectively shackled, Celtic were limited in getting the ball forward to the front men. Eventually they came to rely on the accurate distribution of Alan Stubbs, who was able to bypass the midfield with a succession of long balls.

Despite the endeavour on both sides, and Hearts certainly seemed to be putting more into the game than Celtic, the two goalkeepers had relatively quiet matches. This was a game of last-minute tackles and desperate blocking, rather than clear-cut shooting chances. Hearts perhaps felt that Stubbs should have been sent off for serious foul play in the sixtieth minute. The defender was pursuing Neil McCann who had raced on to a loose ball when the Hearts winger tumbled to the ground. There was definitely contact but Stubbs was equally adamant that McCann had made the most of a fairly harmless challenge. Fortunately, Tom Boyd was between Stubbs and the goal which meant Stubbs was not the last man and escaped with a yellow card.

Just before the Stubbs incident, Celtic had been struck a cruel blow when McNamara limped off in the fiftieth minute to be replaced by Donnelly. Without the midfield guile and strong running of McNamara, Celtic's attacking potential was further limited. But there was worse to come when, in 74 minutes, Mahé and Hamilton collided and the Frenchman had to be stretchered off with a badly injured knee. The concern was plainly etched on Jansen's face as the stretcher passed him on the touch-line.

By this stage Celtic seemed to realise that it was not going to be their day. Even so they came close, as they had done before, to pulling an improbable victory out of the hat. Right on the stroke of full time the ball broke to Simon Donnelly who struck a magnificent shot, but Rousset denied him with an equally magnificent save. It was that kind of day.

The Celtic fans trooped away disconsolate at two more points dropped, two star players injured, and their misery was complete with the news of a 3–2 win for Rangers against Dunfermline. Celtic were still level with Hearts but Rangers were now ominously only three points behind, with the next Old Firm league fixture being only a fortnight away.

Celtic 0   Hearts 0

Celtic: Gould, Boyd, Rieper, Stubbs, Mahé, McNamara, Burley, Lambert, Wieghorst, Brattbakk, Larsson

Substitutes: Donnelly for McNamara, Jackson for Brattbakk, Hannah for Mahé

Bookings: Rieper, Stubbs

Attendance: 50,038

THE TREBLE VANISHES

Kilmarnock v Celtic
8 April 1998

Celtic were now going into one of the most crucial seven-day periods of their season. In that week they would face Rangers twice – once in the league, once in the Scottish Cup – as well as facing a difficult away trip to Kilmarnock, which had so often been the grave of their title ambitions. The games were difficult enough in themselves but they would have to do it without some of their key players. Stephane Mahé's injury would keep him out for at least the rest of the season, while the combination of the ankle injury and tendonitis in the knee would mean McNamara would also be unavailable for a couple of weeks.

These injuries were bad enough but the injury to Mahé was something of an ill omen for Celtic. The French defender had settled in superbly at Celtic Park. He was solid in defence and, as the season wore on and he grew in confidence, his attacking skills came more into play. He had even chipped in with a vital goal against Dunfermline. But Mahé was also something of a talisman for the Celtic side. He had yet to finish a game on a losing side. He missed the early season defeats against Hibs and Dunfermline, was suspended for the defeat by Motherwell and when they lost to St Johnstone he was injured. The closest he came to losing was in the first Old Firm game, but he didn't finish that one because he was sent off before the end. By this stage of the season, when augurs and omens are seen in almost everything, the loss of Stephane Mahé was doubly significant.

In addition to their injury problems, Celtic also had Morten Wieghorst unavailable for the Scottish Cup semi-final thanks to a bit of lip to the referee in the dying seconds of the quarter-final against Dundee United. Regi Blinker was fit again, however, and although there was some doubt over Paul Lambert he too had declared himself fit.

Although the game is traditionally played at a neutral venue, the unavailability of Hampden because of reconstruction meant Celtic and Rangers drew lots for the venue. Celtic 'won' and the game went ahead at Celtic Park with the crowd being divided more or less 50-50.

Celtic will look back on the match and think that it was a game that they should have won and won comfortably. Once again Goram was in great form as he denied the Celtic forwards on several occasions. Larsson and Burley both forced great saves from Goram in the first 20 minutes. Celtic came even closer when, with Goram beaten, an O'Donnell header flew across the face of the goal requiring only the faintest of touches to put it over the line. No touch came and Rangers survived.

Despite a weakened midfield, which included Lambert and Burley both carrying injuries and O'Donnell in his first start since October, Celtic had taken a grip on the game. They dominated the first half and the early part of the second, but with the score still goalless the fans started to become uneasy. You could really only miss so many chances against Rangers, and Celtic seemed to have used up their entitlement. The turning point came in 68 minutes when an injury to Stubbs forced the big defender to leave the field. The loss of Stubbs came at a point when Rangers were starting to come into the game and Gould had been forced into a number of excellent saves. With a reorganised defence and Rangers starting to scent that there might be something in this game for them, the goal was not long in coming. In 74 minutes Jorg Albertz, unmarked out on the left, crossed the ball into the Celtic six-yard box where McCoist – who had made a run – was picked up and scored with a diving header. Thirteen minutes later Albertz himself made it two when he ran unchallenged past a number of defenders before striking an unstoppable shot past Gould. Two minutes later Burley side-footed into the net from close range, but the game was well beyond Celtic at this stage. The Treble dream had been dashed and it would be Rangers going on to the Scottish Cup final against Hearts.

For keeper Jonathan Gould it was the low point of the season.

'Getting knocked out by Rangers didn't go down well,' he admitted. 'But I think it hurt more when I watched the final between them and Hearts. That's when it hit me that this was the last game of the season and we could have been playing for the Treble.'

The Cup defeat by Rangers left Celtic on their knees physically and emotionally. Sheer physical tiredness had played a significant part in the defeat, but now they were going to have to pick themselves up from that Sunday disappointment and face Kilmarnock at Rugby Park. Celtic had won only twice in their last eight visits to Rugby Park and those results had cost them dearly. A 2–0 defeat at the same time during the previous season had just about finished off Celtic's chances of preventing Rangers from winning their ninth league title in a row and equalling Celtic's proud record. That apart, the team which faced Kilmarnock would be even more depleted than the one which lost to Rangers in the Cup. Even though Wieghorst was back from suspension, Alan Stubbs had now joined Mahé and McNamara on the injury list.

This had all the makings of a nervous 90 minutes for Celtic and life was not made easier by deplorable conditions – the cold wind and the driving rain were more suited to December than April. This was a game where Celtic would be required to strain every nerve and sinew if they were to become champions. There wasn't a man on the Celtic side who wasn't aware that this was a game where the title could be won or lost. The fixture was being played in midweek because of the Cup game the previous weekend, but there was added pressure in the fact that Rangers had chosen to play their rearranged game before the Cup tie. They had beaten Hibs and had now turned the psychological screws by being level with Celtic on points. Had Celtic lost to Kilmarnock, Rangers would have gone back to the top of the league.

With so much riding on the game Celtic started patiently and Kilmarnock, who were in the hunt for points for European qualification, were in no mood to chase the game. Celtic were looking more positive as the game progressed and, in the twentieth minute, they took a deserved lead. Phil O'Donnell seemed to be revelling in his role in the left side of midfield, and after beating a Kilmarnock defender, he spotted Larsson running into the box.

O'Donnell's cross was expertly judged and Larsson met it perfectly to send the ball in a shallow parabola which eluded Gordon Marshall and ended up in the net. Kilmarnock battled back and felt hard done by when Gary Holt was barged to the ground inside the Celtic area. Celtic, for their part, could point to a number of questionable offside decisions that so incensed Wim Jansen he had to be spoken to by the match officials.

Kilmarnock did get an equaliser before half-time with a goal which recalled Donnelly's equaliser against Dundee United. This time it was Wright who unleashed a fierce shot which Gould did well to stop, but Burke ran in to fire it home from an acute angle. With the conditions deteriorating and the pitch turning into a mud bath, Kilmarnock started to look sharper, especially at the start of the second half. But, just when things looked like they were going against them, Donnelly contributed what might have been his best goal of the season. O'Donnell, Larsson,

Simon Donnelly ends a breathtaking move by chipping in the winner in the vital 2–1 victory at Kilmarnock

Darren Jackson celebrates triumph over Kilmarnock in a fixture which has cost Celtic dearly in the past

Burley and then Jackson had combined in a sublime passing move to get the ball to the young forward at the edge of the box. Donnelly could have snatched at it but he kept his cool and, with the audacity of youth, he scored a goal that was worthy of the build-up when he chipped the ball over Marshall's head and into the net.

Even though there was more than half an hour to go, the game was won. Jackson had a shot superbly saved by Marshall only a moment later. The former Celtic keeper also denied both Donnelly and Wieghorst and managed to stop a defeat becoming a rout. Nonetheless, the damage had been done and Celtic were back on top of the league. A week which had started badly seemed to be picking up a little.

Celtic 2   Kilmarnock 1
Larsson   Burke
Donnelly

Celtic: Gould, Boyd, Annoni, Rieper, Donnelly, O'Donnell, Burley, Lambert, Wieghorst, Larsson, Jackson

Substitutes: None

Bookings: Wieghorst

Attendance: 18,076

SUNDAY BLUES

Rangers v Celtic
12 April 1998

It had all looked so different a month before. As Celtic lined up to face Dundee United they were relishing the prospect of a seven-point lead over Rangers. The amateur mathematicians had worked out that, with results going in their favour, the league could be won on Easter Sunday. Now here it was and things had gone slightly awry. Another Sunday televised game saw Celtic travelling to Ibrox a good deal more nervous than they needed to be. Rangers had been the form team over the past month, with Celtic now defending a slender three-point lead and with it the realisation that Rangers could be top of the league by the end of the day. Some of the pessimists among the Celtic Park faithful could also point to the fact that Celtic hadn't won a televised Sunday game all season.

Rangers had won the league for the past nine seasons and seemed to have only woken up to the fact that they might be about to lose their most cherished possession. Their team was ageing and fragile in key areas, but they had built up a winning habit which was a powerful psychological barrier in their favour. This title was really now more of a mental battle than a physical one and it would all come down to team spirit and the will to win. Hearts had, surprisingly, lost 2–1 to bottom club Hibs in the Edinburgh derby and, with only four games left to play, they seemed to have shot their bolt. Now it was down to the big two, and Celtic would have to step up to the mark and prove that they wanted this title badly enough to win it.

Once again there were injury problems. Wieghorst had picked up a knock against Kilmarnock and would not play. Mahé, of course, was still out but there were hopes that McNamara might make some kind of return. Agonisingly, for the player and the club, after training successfully all week, he injured his ankle again in the very last minute of the final training session for the Rangers game. There were also concerns over Darren Jackson who was suffering from a chest complaint. Despite coughing and spluttering for most of that Easter Sunday morning, Jackson declared himself fit; a decision which would have serious repercussions very quickly.

The strain of what had been a long season was very obviously beginning to tell on a Celtic squad which was talented but limited; they were good enough, but were there enough of them to do the job? Craig Burley, for example, had been playing on despite what amounted to sciatica. Even with his injuries he had turned out in 43 games so far this season.

'I don't feel as sharp as at the start of the season,' said Burley. 'But I will grind it out with the rest of the lads.'

This was, indeed, shaping up to be a title which would have to be won with rolled-up sleeves rather than silky skills, and the first hurdle was Rangers. Celtic began the game confidently enough, controlling the midfield and picking out their attackers with telling passes. Larsson, who was plainly nearing exhaustion at times, seemed to be energising his runs through sheer force of will, but they were still enough to cause problems for the Rangers defence. But, almost as Celtic were settling into a pattern of dominance from which they could build, their plans were thrown into chaos. Jackson, who had declared himself fit after the warm-up, was plainly toiling on the pitch. He could not catch his breath and, in 23 minutes, he had to be taken off and replaced by Brattbakk. This was a telling blow for Celtic. Apart from the fact that Brattbakk's goal-scoring form had shaded after that purple patch in February, Jackson's more combative style was more suited to this game than the Norwegian's diagonal runs.

As Celtic were reorganising things after Jackson's substitution they were dealt a body blow. A Rangers attack was cleared and the header dropped for Jonas Thern some 25 yards out. Thern met the ball perfectly on the full and smashed an unstoppable volley past Gould for one of the goals of the season. This was a game where the heads could not go down and Celtic rallied immediately. Paul Lambert began to demonstrate a fine combination of skill and aggression as he came

Lambert beat Lorenzo Amoruso and Andy Goram but the ball went past the goal in one of Celtic's best chances of the game

forward from his usual defensive midfield role. He had three shots in succession, any one of which might have gone in. The best of them, on the half hour, beat Goram but slid inches past the post.

Despite their early midfield dominance and the shots from Lambert and Jackson (before he went off) Celtic had still to bring a save of any note from Andy Goram. When he was tested, by a combination of Stubbs and Rieper, he was more than capable of dealing with whatever Celtic had to throw at him. In truth, by this stage, the Celtic arsenal was beginning to look rather depleted. This was a game which was highlighting Celtic's faults rather than showcasing their virtues. With Brattbakk not making any headway, they lacked the cutting edge to score against a solid, if uninspired, Rangers defence. Equally, with

Rangers prepared to soak up pressure, Celtic were missing someone with sufficient midfield guile to break down the defenders and release the strikers.

As the game wore on Celtic started to tire and they were caught once again by their biggest defensive failing. The Celtic defence were susceptible to a determined player who was prepared to run directly at them and take them on. Steve McManaman had proved that in the first Liverpool game, and Jorg Albertz had proved it again at Celtic Park just a week before. On both occasions neither man was tackled and on each occasion they went on to score. History repeated itself in 65 minutes when Jorg Albertz picked the ball up wide and about 40 yards out from the Celtic goal. Just as the previous week, he ran towards the defence, just as the previous week, the defenders backed off, and just as the

The title race was as close as this duel between Phil O'Donnell and Ally McCoist in the final Old Firm league encounter of the season

previous week he buried the ball in the back of the net. This time he was even allowed time to check and take a touch to line it up for his favoured left foot before scoring. It was a dreadful goal for Celtic to lose, made all the more dreadful for being a carbon copy of the goal the week before.

With Rangers 2–0 up, an exhausted Celtic had no real answer. The home side ran riot and it was only sloppy finishing from Ally McCoist as much as anything else which kept the final score down. Even so, a 2–0 win was enough to claw back Celtic's three-point lead and put Rangers top of the league on goal difference of a single goal.

After the game Wim Jansen summed up the task facing his tired team.

'We know that we now have to win our remaining four games if we are to win the league. But the four teams we have to play also need to win. We also have to remember that it could go to goal difference, so we will have to try to score a lot of goals.'

It was a simple enough task on paper, but now the fans were beginning to wonder if the team was going to have the physical and mental stamina to carry it out.

Celtic 0   Rangers 2
                           Thern
                           Albertz

Celtic: Gould, Annoni, Stubbs, Rieper, Boyd, Donnelly, Burley, Lambert, O'Donnell, Larsson, Jackson

Substitutes: Brattbakk for Jackson

Bookings: Annoni, Larsson, O'Donnell

Attendance: 50,042

BACK ON TOP

Motherwell v Celtic
18 April 1998

Anyone looking at the league fixture list when it was released back in the summer of 1997, might have worked out that the last few games of the season might be decisive in determining who won the title. They could not possibly have predicted just how important these games would be. No one could have foreseen that Celtic and Rangers would go into these final matches with only a single goal between them and everything to play for in the race for the flag.

On paper Rangers seemed to have the harder task, since their run-in included Aberdeen, Hearts and Dundee United away from home, as well as Kilmarnock at Ibrox. Celtic, on the other hand, had three home ties against Motherwell, Hibs and St Johnstone with only one away match, Dunfermline. From Celtic's point of view, however, not one of these was an easy match. It was not only tight at the top, it was tight all over the division with everything to play for right up to the end. Motherwell, Hibs and Dunfermline had spent most of the season in the bottom reaches of the league and all of them could yet be relegated. St Johnstone, on the other hand, were in the happy position of challenging for fourth spot in the league which would give them a UEFA Cup place. Everyone had something to play for, but none more so than Celtic.

Wim Jansen had characterised his four remaining matches as four Cup finals and in that sense he was quite correct. But if Celtic were to do what he wanted them to do, then that would involve something they had not done since February – win two matches in succession. Since the 5–1 win over Dunfermline on 25 February and the 1–0 win against Hibs on 28 February, Celtic had not won two league games back to back. It was this level of inconsistency which had allowed a Rangers side who were also dogged by erratic play back into the title race.

Crucially, for the vital four game run-in Jansen had pretty much a full squad to choose from. With the obvious exception of long-term injuries to Mahé and Tommy Johnson, Jansen had his whole squad fit and free from suspension. Even though McNamara was able to play, Jansen allowed himself the luxury of starting him on the bench along with Wieghorst and a fully fit Blinker. Jackson, who had recovered from his viral complaint, partnered Larsson and Donnelly in a three-man attack, while Harald Brattbakk was omitted from the squad.

Celtic started the game as nervously as you might expect and nowhere was this more evident than in defence. With the Rangers game against Aberdeen being played the following day, Celtic had the chance to go back to the top of the league with an emphatic win. But their nervy start didn't inspire the fans with any confidence. The uncharacteristic sight of the normally immaculate Rieper conceding possession needlessly was a sign of the nerves in the Celtic defence. Motherwell, with new Finnish manager Harri Kampmann making his first visit to Celtic Park in a competitive situation, started in a much more relaxed frame of mind. They looked confident and were full of running, and it came more as a shock than as a surprise when they took the lead in 12 minutes. Alan Stubbs, this time, was the man who gave away possession and Motherwell's Stephen McMillan proceeded to carve his way through the Celtic defence. He managed to get the ball to Shivute whose shot was blocked and while Celtic tried to decide who was going to clear it, it bounced towards McMillan who gratefully stuck it into the net.

The huge shirt-sleeved crowd were stunned, especially since Larsson and Jackson had already gone close for Celtic. This was now going to be a game where Celtic would have to stand up and be counted if they were to win Wim his four Cup finals. By this stage of the season they knew enough not to chase the game and continued to play patiently, with controlled football and retaining possession wherever possible. Yard by yard they took the game to Motherwell, forcing the Lanarkshire side onto the back foot. The fans sensed that an equaliser was in the offing. It came when Boyd sent O'Donnell clear on the left and the born-again midfielder was off like a hare. When he hit the byline and cut the ball back into the Motherwell box, Burley was standing eight yards out to smack it home.

Once Celtic got back on level terms it seemed inevitable that they would go on to win. Burley had complained of being tired lately but there was no sign of it in this game. A powerful Celtic midfield overran Motherwell and – but for the heroics of Brian Martin in central defence – they would have added to their score more quickly. As it was, it took until the 43rd minute for Celtic to go into the lead. Stubbs unleashed a devastating 60-yard pass from defence which sailed over the heads of the midfield and seemed destined for Larsson. With his back to the goal and the attentive Martin standing behind him, Larsson elected to kill the ball on his chest, allowing it to drop for Burley. It took only a few steps for Burley to gather the ball, compose himself and send a 20-yard shot screaming past Stevie Woods into the Motherwell net. This was Burley's fifteenth goal of the season, a telling contribution from midfield in a Celtic side which seemed to be able to score goals from almost anywhere.

Jansen had stressed to his players the potential importance of goal difference in settling the destination of the title. That being the case, there was no question of Celtic sitting back on their lead in the second half. They continued to come at the Motherwell defence in waves as they sought to improve their position. Five minutes into the second half they made it three with a marvellous piece of understanding which again involved that man Burley. It was Burley who broke out of the midfield and reached the edge of the box before spotting Jackson, who was well placed at the back post. Burley hoisted a well-aimed cross which found Jackson who then, instead of going for goal himself, took the pace off the ball with a delicate header and allowed it to drop for Simon Donnelly to stroke into the net.

Five minutes later Donnelly struck again and, once more, it was goalscorer Burley who turned provider in a piece of breathtaking skill. This time the move began with Larsson who raced down the left in a dangerous run before knocking the ball inside to Burley. The midfielder was aware of Simon Donnelly making a lung-bursting run and he knew all he had to do was knock a gentle reverse pass into his path. Donnelly never missed a stride as he took the ball to send it flying past Stevie Woods – who was fortunate enough to get a hand to it without ever hoping to stop it.

It was a fine afternoon for Celtic, but by far the biggest cheer of the day came when Darren Jackson was substituted in 82 minutes. Jackson had played tirelessly and the crowd showed generous appreciation, but the biggest ovation was reserved for the man coming on in Jackson's place. Jackie McNamara was back and he did enough in the eight minutes he was on the field to show how badly he had been missed, and also how much he could contribute to the three remaining 'Cup finals'.

Celtic had done everything that Wim Jansen had asked of them. They had gained three points and they had scored a few goals in the process. Twenty-four hours later Rangers would not be up to the job against Aberdeen and defeat at Pittodrie would leave Celtic back on top – three points clear and three games to go.

Celtic 4   Motherwell 1

Burley (2)   McMillan

Donnelly (2)

Celtic: Gould, Annoni, Stubbs, Rieper, Boyd, Lambert, Burley, O'Donnell, Donnelly, Larsson, Jackson

Substitutes: McNamara for Jackson

Bookings: None

Attendance: 49,541

FIRING BLANKS

Hibs v Celtic
25 April 1998

There was no question that the pressure was starting to tell on Celtic as they came to within 270 minutes of the title. But things were tough all over and the pressure wasn't only being felt at Celtic Park. There was a psychological war being waged all over the Premier Division. Sources at Ibrox let it be known that they felt that Celtic had blown it after squandering what could have been a seven-point advantage. And the war of nerves was not confined to the top of the league.

Alex McLeish has always been regarded as one of the brightest of Scotland's young managers. Towards the end of the season he had swapped clubs, moving from Motherwell who were second bottom, to Hibs who were bottom, in a move which brought to mind comparisons involving frying pans and fires. McLeish's sole responsibility, as he and his board saw it, was to make sure that Hibs stayed in the top flight by any means necessary. Going into this game Hibs were firmly on the bottom, five points adrift of Dunfermline and with rapidly dwindling options. That can be the only reason for the bit of pop psychology which McLeish attempted on the morning of the game. Celtic fans woke up to see the back pages of the newspapers full of earnest pleading from McLeish to match referee George Clyde. The manager sincerely hoped that Mr Clyde would not be swayed in decisions which could have huge repercussions for both clubs by the 50,000 rampant home fans. Apart from being an obvious bit of kidology on McLeish's part, to suggest that George Clyde would be influenced by the crowd was an unwarranted slur on a referee of many years' standing.

In the end, McLeish's statements seemed to have been unnecessary since Mr Clyde had what might best be termed an erratic game. There were many strange decisions and most of them favoured Hibs. None was stranger than an incident towards the end of the first half when Hibs winger Tony Rougier appeared to elbow Simon Donnelly in the face, was then tackled by Enrico Annoni and Annoni was the one who ended up with the booking.

Refereeing decisions apart there was not a lot to get excited about in this game. Celtic were looking for the back-to-back wins which had eluded them for two months and which would have made life a lot more comfortable for them. They played, however, as if they wanted the points to be dropped in their lap. At times the Celtic side seemed paralysed with nerves, and with Hibs desperate to avoid losing a goal, this was not an attractive spectacle.

The first real action came at the Hibs end in 20 minutes. Darren Dods had intercepted a through ball from Alan Stubbs intended for Henrik Larsson. But, with the danger apparently clear, he then under-hit his pass back to Bryan Gunn in the Hibs goal thus allowing Larsson to nip in. It was the sort of chance a sharper Larsson would have buried earlier in the season; now he chipped the keeper, but the ball went over Gunn and wide of the post. This was really the only thing which Gunn had to do in the first half, and Gould did even less as Hibs attacked without ever causing any real problems.

Whatever Wim Jansen said to his players at half-time seemed to have done the trick, because when they came out for the second half Celtic played with a good deal more purpose. They threatened almost immediately from the restart and Craig Burley went close with a long-range shot which went over the bar. Celtic continued to look threatening and appeared to be about to take the lead in 53 minutes. A long ball out of defence found Simon Donnelly in the centre-circle, timing his run to get on the end of it. With Donnelly racing forward and only the keeper to beat, the opening goal seemed certain until Mr Clyde blew for offside. The decision incensed everyone – except of course the small Hibs contingent – since Donnelly appeared to have been in his own half when the ball was played and therefore could not have been offside. Television replays appeared to suggest it was a borderline call but, even so, Donnelly should have been given the benefit of the doubt. Twenty minutes later Donnelly had another chance to settle the issue with a diving header after Larsson's shot had been punched out by

Gunn. The young forward missed when it would have appeared easier to score. It plainly wasn't Donnelly's day; just a minute earlier he had had a shot cleared off the line by Willie Miller with Gunn helpless.

Celtic were having the better of the play but still could not break down a stubborn Hibs defence. Anyone who needed an example of the tension involved in this fixture had only to watch Alex McLeish and Celtic's assistant coach Murdo MacLeod being sent off for a verbal clash on the touch-line. Passions were running high on the field as the moments ticked away. Six minutes from the end Celtic appeared to have been denied a penalty when Bryan Gunn dropped the ball and Hibs defender John Hughes plainly tripped O'Donnell as he attempted to pounce on the loose ball.

Jansen had sent on McNamara, Wieghorst and Blinker as Celtic tried to get forward to score the goal which had eluded them. Blinker was only on for the last ten minutes, but he appeared to make a difference. First he linked up well with McNamara, but the young midfielder was ruled offside; then, with almost the last kick of the game, Blinker sent in a fierce shot which Miller – once again the Hibs hero – cleared off the line.

In fairness, Celtic should have won this game. In spite of being nervy and hesitant they had done enough to score at least once. But football has nothing to do with fairness, which is why the Celtic fans left under a cloud and the Hibs fans left jubilant to have staved off relegation. The Hibs celebrations would be short-lived since they would be formally relegated the following Saturday. For Celtic the situation had got even worse. While they were drawing with Hibs in Glasgow, Rangers had beaten Hearts in Edinburgh. This effectively finished Hearts' challenge and they could reasonably reflect that they had lost the league because of their inability to beat either member of the Old Firm. They would, however, get their revenge on Rangers with a magnificent performance to win the Scottish Cup.

The Rangers victory meant that the gap between the two teams was now down to one point. Rangers were playing the following Saturday, Celtic had another televised Sunday game. No one at Celtic Park needed to be told that if Rangers won on the Saturday, Celtic would be under incalculable pressure the following day.

Celtic 0   Hibs 0

Celtic: Gould, Boyd, Stubbs, Rieper, Annoni, Donnelly, Burley, Lambert, O'Donnell, Larsson, Jackson

Substitutes: McNamara for Jackson, Blinker for Donnelly, Wieghorst for Burley

Bookings: Boyd, Annoni

Attendance: 50,034

SEVEN MINUTES

Dunfermline v Celtic
3 May 1998

As Jimmy Greaves often quipped to Ian St John on their late and unlamented Saint and Greavsie TV show, 'It's a funny old game.' Celtic fans had been bracing themselves for a stomach-churning trip to Fife for the game against Dunfermline. As they left Celtic Park the previous Saturday, they were assuming they would have to beat Dunfermline and beat them well, just to take the league to the last day. But what a difference a day makes. Maybe Greavsie had a point after all.

Referee Bobby Tait had added on an unfeasible amount of injury time when Celtic last played Hearts at Tynecastle. The extra time had allowed José Quitongo to score a crazy goal and deny Celtic two vital points. Now, in some sort of karmic irony, his unique sense of timekeeping had done exactly the same thing to Rangers. The Ibrox side were expected to make short work of Kilmarnock at home, especially when they knew a win would put them two points clear at the top of the league. Bizarrely though, as the game ticked towards the 90 minutes, Kilmarnock were holding on for a draw. Ninety minutes came and went and, as referee Tait continued to add time on, Kilmarnock stunned Rangers with a ninety-third-minute winner. The cheers from the teletext watchers and radio listeners in the East End of Glasgow could be heard all over the city.

Rangers had lost. They had apparently fallen at the final hurdle. A win for Celtic against Dunfermline the following day would give the Celtic Park side their first title in ten years. The realisation was enough to send thousands of fans, many of them ticketless, up the motorway to Fife, desperate to be there when the league was won. Ten thousand more crammed into Celtic Park to watch the game as it was beamed back on to a giant video screen in the shadow of the main stand. For hundreds of thousands more it was a case of savouring the moment in front of televisions in pubs, clubs, or the comfort of their own homes. Who cares if Celtic hadn't won a televised Sunday game all season? This time there was an even more powerful omen in their favour. Thirty years ago, almost to the day, Celtic had gone to East End Park needing to beat Dunfermline to win the league. On that occasion they won 2–1 and, to maintain a touch with the past, the current Dunfermline manager Bert Paton was in the Pars side that day.

'There's no doubt that Kilmarnock's result against Rangers was a big boost for us,' said Celtic captain Tom Boyd. 'After that we knew that all we had to do was win one of our last two games and we would win the league.'

Certainly, Boyd's mood appeared to be shared by the rest of the team as they made their way down the steps from the East End Park dressing-room and on to the pitch. So many Celtic fans had made the trip that the noise was almost like a home game for Celtic and the team looked a good deal more relaxed than they had been for weeks. The mood in Dunfermline was matched back in Glasgow where shirt-sleeved fans sang and chanted while they watched the game, secure in the expectation that the day would end with the league trophy being brought back by the conquering heroes.

The party atmosphere at Dunfermline was infectious and quickly spread from the terracings to the team. The previous day's results had meant that Dunfermline were safe from the fear of relegation and had little to play for. Bert Paton, however, had warned that they would not be mere bystanders to a victory procession for Celtic. Despite Paton's public pronouncements, that was pretty much the way things were shaping up on the field. Celtic played relaxed, controlled football and while Dunfermline weren't about to lie down to them, they found it hard to compete against Celtic in their first-half mood. The busiest man in the park was goalkeeper Ian Westwater. The last time he had faced Celtic he had picked the ball out of the net five times and early indications were that Celtic intended to repeat the performance here. Westwater needed to be sharp to save twice from Donnelly, as well as managing to beat out what could have been an own goal from Greg

Shields. But his defences were finally breached in 35 minutes.

Phil O'Donnell tackled his former club-mate Gerry Britton near the centre-circle and he then slipped the ball to Larsson. While O'Donnell had been moving forward, Simon Donnelly had begun his run, and by the time Larsson got the ball he spotted Donnelly and sent the ball perfectly into his path. Westwater came out to narrow the angle but he was always going to be beaten by Donnelly's fine shot. One-nil and in the minds of the Celtic fans, the first of at least a few. While bare-chested fans waved banners and celebrated the Celtic players went about adding to their total. Westwater was in impressive form as he denied Donnelly twice more, as well as turning a Larsson shot round the post.

Wim Jansen had spent most of the first half on the touch-line screaming at officials, but he could not have been unhappy with the way his side had played. They went in at half-time only 45 minutes away from being champions and came out again determined to hang on to that lead. They continued to make chances, but their play lacked the urgency of the first half and they seemed content to try to protect their lead. This is not always the wisest of tactics and its wisdom on this occasion seemed questionable. It could, however, all have been academic but for a questionable refereeing decision in the final quarter of the game. Larsson, who was due a goal for his efforts in this match, raced past two defenders and into the penalty box. But as he got past the last of them, Craig Ireland, he had his jersey pulled and he tumbled to the ground. It was a cynical move by the defender, which television replays showed to have happened inside the box and therefore a stonewall penalty. Referee John Underhill was having none of it and didn't even give a free-kick. A penalty at this stage would have killed the game and won the league – as it was, the denial of a good claim was merely the precursor to disaster for Celtic.

Five minutes later Larsson was again involved when he conceded a free-kick about ten yards into his own half. Dunfermline sent a long and highly speculative lob into the Celtic area and Craig Faulconbridge, a youngster on loan from Coventry City, managed to get his head to it. Faulconbridge didn't hit it cleanly and wasn't able to put any kind of direction on it, but it spun off his head in a high arc which ended up by going over the head of Jonathan Gould and into the back of the net. The only thing Jonathan Gould had had to do all day was pick that ball out of the net.

The Dunfermline fans were jubilant, the Celtic fans at East End Park were stunned, those at Celtic Park let out howls of anguish as their dream was snatched away from them. Jansen put on Brattbakk and Wieghorst in an attempt to step up the pace but he had waited far too long. They should have been on much earlier to give his tired forwards some respite and put Dunfermline under fresh pressure. Despite a late flurry the game was over.

Celtic had been seven minutes away from the title. Now they were going to have to go back to Celtic Park the following Saturday and win. Anything else could let Rangers steal the league at the last gasp.

Celtic 1   Dunfermline 1
Donnelly   Faulconbridge

Celtic: Gould, Boyd, Annoni, McNamara, Rieper, Stubbs, Larsson, Burley, Donnelly, Lambert, O'Donnell

Substitutes: Wieghorst for O'Donnell, Brattbakk for McNamara

Bookings: Annoni

Attendance: 12,866

1Ø IN A ROW

St Johnstone v Celtic
9 May 1998

So it was all down to this; one last throw of the dice on the final day of the season.

Celtic had to beat St Johnstone at home to make certain of winning the league. Any other result could allow Rangers, who were playing Dundee United at Tannadice, to win the league by a clear points margin or on goal difference. The title race was so tight that the league trophy was being put into a helicopter which would take off at the beginning of the second half of each game and then hover until the destination of the trophy was decided. This last 90 minutes of the season would either be the stuff of fondest dreams or darkest nightmares.

Since the end of February, Celtic supporters had been feeling rather like Moses in the wilderness. They were allowed to see the promised land but would, like him, never be allowed inside. Over the past few weeks Celtic fans had seen so many tantalising glimpses of the promised land of the league title, but still they lacked a Joshua to lead them over the threshold. Those who turned up at Celtic Park on 9 May were nervous but generally optimistic. St Johnstone still had an outside chance of qualifying for the UEFA Cup if they beat Celtic so it was not going to be easy, but beating the Saints was something that a decent Celtic side should accomplish 99 times out of 100. The statistically minded would point out that a St Johnstone win on the last Saturday of the year would mean they had had their turn as far as the law of averages was concerned.

All roads led to Celtic Park that Saturday afternoon in May. London Road, Gallowgate and points in between were a sea of green and white as 50,000 fans trooped along to join – what they hoped – was going to be the party of the decade. Thousands more who did not have tickets came along anyway to stand outside the ground listening to the game on their radios and guessing at the roars and cheers coming from within. The media were out in force too. Everywhere you looked there were small knots of Celtic supporters in green and white face paint and green, white and gold Harpo wigs, obliging yet another camera crew with a rendition of 'The Celtic Song'. Inside the ground the crowd were doing their best to live up to Wim Jansen's exhortation in the match programme. He urged the crowd, which has so often been described as 'Celtic's twelfth man', to take that job seriously and roar their team on to the title. The fans obliged and chorus after chorus of 'The Celtic Song', 'You'll Never Walk Alone', the plaintive 'Fields of Athenry', and the newly adopted but fondly embraced 'Roll With It' soared up and into the afternoon air. By the time the players came out in earnest their supporters' throats were raw but still, as Celtic went into the traditional pre-game huddle, the noise could have been heard by the thousands of Rangers fans who had gathered at Ibrox to watch a beam-back of their match against Dundee United.

For all of this though, there was still a game to be won. Recently, Celtic seemed to feel the pressure of their fans more acutely at home than they did away, and there had been some hesitant performances. This was a game where Celtic could not allow themselves to be caught cold. An early goal was the order of the day and, for once, the game went according to the script. Henrik Larsson picked up the ball wide on the left-hand side of the pitch. He kept control and, as he looked for options, he drifted along the line of Saints defenders. Everyone thought he was waiting for Donnelly – or even Burley – to get into a shooting position. But as he evaded a third tackle, he knocked the ball slightly to his right, made a little space for himself and unleashed a devastating shot which curled and dipped behind the diving Alan Main. Two minutes gone, Celtic a goal up, time for more effort from those raw throats.

The goal was exactly what Celtic and the crowd needed. Their play was as composed as possible – under the circumstances – and they began to come forward. They had learned their lesson of the previous week and there was no question of even trying to sit on a one-goal lead for 88 minutes. Shots rained in from all quarters on Alan Main and his defenders – even Rico Annoni forced a save from Main with a right-footed shot. But, through a combination of unlucky finishing, heroic

The goal that started the party: Henrik Larsson caps a glorious season with the opening goal against St Johnstone

defending and undoubted skill on the part of the young Saints keeper, it remained at 1–0 at the break. St Johnstone were lucky not to go in level when an unmarked George O'Boyle managed to head over the bar from six yards out just before half-time.

The score at Tannadice was also 1–0, to Rangers. If both scores stayed the same at the end of 90 minutes then the title was Celtic's. The lesson of Dunfermline was still in their minds and the Celtic players knew an equaliser for St Johnstone could give the league to Rangers.

Celtic came out for the second half knowing the second goal was vital, but also knowing they could not afford to concede anything. The tension which was evident in their play in the early part of the second half probably seeped down from the terracing – where fans with trannies were able to announce that Rangers had now gone two up.

While all this was happening at Tannadice, St Johnstone were coming more into the game at Celtic Park. Jansen, unlike the previous week, rung the changes early. Donnelly had run himself into the ground and in 59 minutes he was taken off and replaced by Brattbakk. For the next ten minutes St Johnstone continued to press and Celtic were looking on the ropes. Paul Lambert's defensive midfield skills were tested to the limit, but Celtic were still capable of hitting on the break. In the sixty-ninth minute Tom Boyd sent a touch-line-hugging pass down the right to Jackie McNamara, who was already behind the Saints defence by the time the ball reached him. He looked across to see Brattbakk racing into the penalty box with no one near him. McNamara squared the ball and Brattbakk – who had managed to miss softer chances this season – met it perfectly to side-foot it into the net.

It was 4.28 p.m. on Saturday, 9 May 1998. Celtic had won the league.

The game went on, but nothing could be heard above the chorus of songs which rang out from all around the ground. This was the moment they had all waited for. Outside the mood was exactly the same. Men wept, strangers embraced, bottles were shared. It was like VE Day all over again.

Celtic were now on the brink of the unimaginable. The team that had lost their first two games and given everyone six points of a start were now rewriting the record books to become league champions. Jonathan Gould, who had been busier than he might have anticipated in this game, was ideally placed to contemplate the situation.

'I had read in the newspapers that a helicopter would bring the league championship trophy,' he remembers. 'I don't know if it was that helicopter or not but with about ten minutes to go, we were 2–0 up and I looked up and saw a helicopter, and that really brought home to me that the Championship was coming to Celtic Park. We had a couple of hairy moments in the game, but a lot of football is about nerves and how you hold up, and on the day we held up as a team.'

The rest of the game was played out to rising crescendos of 'The Celtic Song' and 'You'll Never Walk Alone' once again, as well as a cheery, if ungrammatical ditty modelled on Rolf Harris's 'Tie Me Kangaroo Down, Sport' which went along the lines of Who's the Champions Now? Under these conditions it was almost impossible for

Jackie McNamara came back from injury to play an important part in the title run-in

the players on the pitch to even hear themselves think. Once the 90 minutes was up, referee Kenny Clark didn't even try to make himself heard above the din. He simply picked up the ball and ended the game. In the process he started a party which went on for days and days in some quarters.

The Celtic celebrations were every bit as intense. The players sported special T-shirts with '1Ø in a Row' on some of them. Others bore the cryptic slogan 'Smell the Glove' – an in-joke which the players still refuse to explain. Captain Tom Boyd, wearing a green and white jester's cap, clung to the league championship trophy as if it were life itself. As the trophy was passed along the line to the rest of a jubilant squad they each realised how much it meant to the club and to the millions of supporters all over the world.

'That was probably the best day I've had in football up till now,' said Alan Stubbs, who had been a rock at the centre of the Celtic defence all season. 'I've played in a Cup final at Wembley and I've won championships with Bolton, but the atmosphere that day is still vivid in my memory now and it will never go away.'

Henrik Larsson, who scored the goal that started it all off, was equally moved by the occasion.

'I just can't describe how I feel but the supporters have waited a long time for this,' he said. 'I have never scored a goal like that in my life. I scored with a penalty in the World Cup but this was by far the most important of my career. I think we've knocked that theory about

Above left: *Jackie McNamara ended his season by picking up one of Scotland's Player of the Year awards*

Above right: *Smell the glove?*

Below: *You'll never walk alone*

1Ø in a row: O'Donnell, Annoni, Stubbs, Boyd and Hannah celebrate

Opposite page (from left to right): *Phil O'Donnell and son turn the title celebrations into a family affair, Marc Rieper applauds the Parkhead faithful who have endured a ten-year wait for the title to return, the League trophy takes pride of place as the singing continues long after the game has ended*

foreigners not playing for the jersey on the head,' said Larsson of the Celtic Park branch of football's Foreign Legion. 'I did this for myself, my team-mates, the back-room staff and the fans.'

Craig Burley, who had become the heart and soul of Celtic during the season, was delighted that the league had finally been won, but even more delighted that it had been won here.

'It was never going to be easy,' he said, 'but we took it to the last day of the season and, with hindsight, I think it was best to win it here at Celtic Park. Yes, it would have been nice to take the title at Dunfermline, but maybe it was meant to happen this way.'

The Celtic celebrations embraced everyone connected with the club. The unfortunate Tommy Johnson was there, proving that his knee could certainly stand up to a bit of celebratory dancing. So too was Stephane Mahé. And so also were the kids as the title celebrations crossed generations. Phil O'Donnell did his lap of honour with his baby son Christopher on his shoulders. Other players brought their kids out and even Wim Jansen's children joined in the singing and the capering.

It was that kind of day, but then Celtic have always been that kind of club.

Celtic 2   St Johnstone 0
Larsson
Brattbakk

Celtic: Gould, Boyd, Annoni, McNamara, Rieper, Stubbs, Larsson, Burley, Donnelly, Lambert, O'Donnell

Substitutes: Wieghorst for O'Donnell, Brattbakk for Donnelly, Blinker for Larsson

Bookings: None

Attendance: 50,032

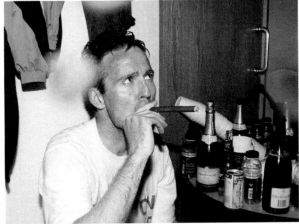

THE AFTERMATH

The party which began at 28 minutes past four on 9 May went on in the East End of Glasgow for days. But while Celtic fans were still celebrating their triumph events behind the scenes cast a shadow over the festivities.

On Monday, 11 May just 48 hours after winning the league Wim Jansen and Celtic parted company. The Dutchman had chosen to activate the get-out clause in his contract and left behind a squad he had assembled and coached to their first league title in ten years. Assistant coach Murdo Macleod remained behind but after a few more weeks he followed in Jansen's footsteps.

The relationship between player and coach is a complex one, especially when he is a winning coach. Jansen's decision was certainly felt by his players.

'There were certainly rumours and we knew that everything wasn't as it should have been,' says captain Tom Boyd. 'It was disappointing that we didn't get the chance to really enjoy the summer as champions because of Wim leaving. Everyone predicted that it would be the case but even when you suspect something like that was about to happen, it's still a shock when it does happen.'

For Alan Stubbs, the departure of Jansen was the major disappointment of the season.

Wim Jansen and Murdo MacLeod share a final moment of triumph; Jansen would leave the club within days

'We had a few low points during the season with individual games,' he recalls. 'But we had won the league and it seemed to be over so quickly because of what happened with Wim Jansen and we didn't celebrate it the way we should have.'

The players wanted to put on a bit of a show for their departing coach. They had one more commitment to fulfil in the shape of a friendly against Sporting Lisbon which was part of the deal which had brought Jorge Cadete to Celtic. The game took place on 12 May, the day after Jansen had announced he was resigning. However, any attempt to give Jansen a rousing farewell was not matched by the performance on the pitch. Celtic lost 2–1 in an understandably low-key game in front of just 4,000 spectators.

Despite the departure of their coach it had been a great season for Celtic. They had won the league and the Coca-Cola Cup and their players had been recognised for their abilities. Craig Burley and Jackie McNamara were named Football Writers Player of the Year and Players Player of the Year respectively. On the world stage when Craig Brown took Scotland to France for the World Cup finals it was with a squad which included eight Celtic players. The club's roll of honour was Jonathan Gould, Tom Boyd, Tosh McKinlay, Jackie McNamara, Craig Burley, Paul Lambert, Darren Jackson and Simon Donnelly. They were joined in France by Marc Rieper and Morton Wieghorst who were part of the Danish squad.

In a statement announcing Wim Jansen's resignation, club chairman Fergus McCann paid tribute to the players and everyone else at the club.

'All of this,' he said of the successful season which had just ended, 'was not the result of the efforts of only one season or only one man. I want to pay tribute to all those at the club, especially the players, all of whom have worked so hard for success, some for four years or more.

'Individuals will always come and go, but the legend that is Celtic continues.'

APPENDIX A

The Captain's Part

On 9 May 1998 Tom Boyd became the first Celtic captain in ten years to lift the league championship trophy to the cheers of the massed hordes at Celtic Park. Here he picks the key moments from the season that saw his side march triumphantly to their first title in a decade.

Celtic v St Johnstone, 23 August 1997

When you turn round and see a striker getting the amount of freedom in the box that George O'Boyle got – and he was very close in – you tend to think 'Oh, no'. As soon as he hits it – and this all happens in a fraction of a second – and he hit it very well, you think: 'That's in the back of the net.' Somehow Jonathan Gould's reflexes took the ball away and he saved it. It was absolutely magnificent. That was a turning point. Any incident in a game, whether it's a last-ditch tackle, or a great clearance, or something like that where the game is evenly balanced, which it was in that game, can turn things around. We had lost the last couple of games and we were looking to go into the record books as the worst start of any Celtic side – losing our first three league games – which we didn't want to do. So I suppose that was a turning point for us, in that we could then go on and try to raise our game, and we were fortunate that we got a great goal from Henrik and then Darren scored, and that was a great lift for us. We never really looked back after that game. Wim Jansen obviously had to sort things out quickly after we had lost our first two league games. After a shaky spell, getting that goal helped us control the game. You see a keeper making a great save and you know you've got out of jail and you go on from there. You think you carry your luck but luck didn't have much to do with that one, that was a great save. Goalkeepers have got to get themselves set but, even though Jonathan had got himself set in that space of time, you still see a lot of shots that are struck with such venom that they take the goalkeeper's hand with them. Obviously, Jonathan got a strong hand on it and was able to palm it away. Without a shadow of a doubt, a lot of goalkeepers would never even have got to that shot. In fact I think some would have tried to get out of the way.

Celtic v Liverpool, 16 September 1997

Looking back, I think maybe we did meet Liverpool a bit too early in the season. We might have liked to wait another month or so until we had settled a wee bit. We were under pressure beforehand because in the league we had given six points away at the start of the campaign, which you don't like to do because we had put ourselves under a lot of pressure. But, beating St Johnstone in the League Cup and then beating them again in the league in the space of a few days gave us a bit of confidence going into the game. I think that at the time we weren't at our best and I think that showed in the first half, especially the first 20 minutes when we gave them too much respect. Once we started to get in about them we realised that they weren't as good as they were made out to be, and we were better than the press had made out. It's hard to say what turns a game like that. It could be the simplest of things. Obviously they got the early goal through Michael Owen and then they had a couple of flurries, but they hadn't added to it and you think: 'Well, maybe this is as good as they're going to get because they haven't added another.' It can turn gradually or it can turn on a tackle or a save – like Jonathan against St Johnstone – or a decision by the referee. Little things can get the crowd going and that helps us to change our approach. Obviously, everyone had written us off and said that it was going to be easy for Liverpool but once we did start to find our feet we gave them a game. We totally dominated the second half and limited Liverpool to a couple of saunters up the park. We were much more threatening in the second half than we were in the first. A lot of that had to do with the tactical switch in changing Jackie McNamara's role. Wim used him more as a right winger/midfielder as opposed to a conventional wing-back, where he's just up and down. The goal that he scored was a magnificent strike. He may have been fortunate to get a slight deflection off one of the Liverpool players but the way he struck it, I don't think he's hit a better shot. That was a phenomenal strike and, coming at the time it did, gave us a great lift. We had started the second half quite well but obviously you need goals and that came at the right time to give us that wee boost. That result really helped set us up for the rest of the season because of Liverpool's reputation. Bearing in mind that we were still in a transition period – we had a lot to learn – we had come close to beating a team of Liverpool's quality and pedigree and that was a big game for us.

Celtic v Dundee United, Coca-Cola Cup final, 30 November 1997

This was round about the time when we were playing really well. We played well throughout that tournament and we got to the final without losing a goal, which was an excellent record. For me it was a great honour as captain to lift the trophy, especially since we hadn't lifted it for so long. We also didn't have a great track record in important games at Ibrox. People talk about hoodoos and such, but I don't think that was the case. It only began to prey on our minds in latter years because before that we had a better record at Ibrox than we did at Celtic Park, certainly in league games. It was just that we had a lot of poor performances in crucial matches at Ibrox, but I think we knew it had to change, it was only a matter of time before it turned. Runs of bad luck have to be broken some time and what better time than in the final? When you start to play games you don't take these so-called hoodoos on to the park, it's just a run of bad results. The thing is to get there in the first place, because that's when your luck can turn and that was our first final in a long time. It was really a case of getting there. Dundee United didn't play to their strengths and they let themselves down a little bit on the day, but I think that would take something away from the quality of our performance. At that time we were playing well – possibly playing our best football of the season – and I think if we had come up against anyone we would have won it. It was a great final and we got a great lift from that because we had bagged our first silverware under those circumstances: going to Ibrox and winning the tournament for the first time in 15 years. Winning the Coca-Cola Cup was important because then you start to be called winners. For the long spell that Celtic went through without winning anything, that was always getting thrown up in your face. Obviously that isn't good enough, so this was a delight for everyone concerned.

Celtic v Rangers, 2 January 1998

This was a very big game for us, because if Rangers had won they would have gone seven points clear. We had given them six points of a start at the beginning of the season, so we didn't want to give them any more – not with time running out as you head into the turn of the year. People say that's the time when you really start playing, but I think in Scotland – where there are generally only the two clubs pushing for it – you have to start playing that bit earlier. This year Hearts came in and put up a great fight and it was a good league for that. So the New Year's Day game was important for all those reasons, but also because we needed a victory against Rangers. We hadn't beaten them in ten games and obviously people attach a lot of significance to the New Year's Day game in terms of going on and winning the league. But we needed to win because we hadn't won the previous nine fixtures and people were starting to say we couldn't beat them. Obviously, you have to beat Rangers at some stage and if you look back to the two previous seasons where we failed to beat them, that ultimately cost us the title. If we had managed one victory in the previous two seasons we would have won the league. For us, having got a defeat and a draw against them so far in the season, it was important to beat them. We needed to beat Rangers in a big game, and they don't come much more important than the New Year's Day game. Everyone put in a performance that day, but the game was going along the same lines as countless others: us battering away at the goal and Andy Goram keeping everything out with brilliant saves. It was looking like the same old story where we were playing well but not getting the result but then the pressure paid off in the second half. A lot of these games usually turn on who scores the first goal and this time it was us.

Celtic v Dundee United, 27 January 1998

We were now reaching the stage where, with Hearts and Rangers still in the race, every game was vital and you have to win every game. That was the first time since the 3–2 game against Motherwell that we had gone on to win after being behind. It was a very important game for us, but I was suspended and watched it from one of the boxes. I didn't enjoy that particularly because I don't think any player is a good spectator, you mentally kick every ball from up there. It was a pretty even game and we had had our chances but not taken them and, even though we had played quite well, we had lost a goal. Against Dundee United we seem to have a good record of coming from behind and we have done it on numerous occasions against them. I think this game highlights the fact that throughout the season the boys played with a lot of determination, as well as a great deal of skill. We were determined to fight for everything and not give up till the final whistle. Also, bearing in mind that this was January when we had poor results either side of the Old Firm game – against St Johnstone and Motherwell – it was important not to drop a point. The last thing you want is to go on a poor run of results at that stage of the season.

Celtic v St Johnstone, 9 May 1998

I think at the start of the season you go in with the belief that you're going to win the league. After our first two games it might have been hard to convince some people, but you still have to have that belief as long as you don't drop too far off the pace. Once we won the League Cup and then got to the top of the league for a spell, we were never far away from our aim after that. But you still have to believe that you're good enough to stay up there right to the death. It was only once the second goal went in that you could think: 'Well, I think that's us now, I think we're home and safe.' St Johnstone came out to play us in the second half because they were pushing to get into Europe, so we knew they wouldn't sit and defend because a draw was no good to them. They had to come out and play at some stage but, to be honest, it would have helped us if it had been earlier, instead of us having to try and break them open. We got the goal from Henrik early on, which meant that they had to come out and they did put us under pressure a couple of times, but once we got that second goal it just turned into a celebration. I had played Jackie McNamara through to start the move. I had waited until he timed his run right and I flicked it over the defender and he collected it perfectly. I think Jackie just looked in and saw Harald and played it first time; someone else might have taken a touch and the moment would have been lost. But Jackie hit it and, with his pace, Harald came in on the end of it and finished it beautifully. It was a great move and a great goal. Harald did everything right; he got over the ball, he kept it down, didn't let it sky and once it hit the back of the net it was party time. All I can remember at the end of the game was the sheer joy that everyone felt, probably with a sense of relief because we hadn't finished it the week before at Dunfermline and we had to win that last game. It wasn't just about that game, it was about the whole season. We hadn't won the league in so long and I remember vividly the joy and the relief on everyone's face. We had been down for a long time and now we were champions. People like Peter Grant and Paul McStay used to tell me that winning the league was the best feeling in the world and they were right. It's totally magnificent.

APPENDIX B

The Championship Squad

Jonathan Gould (Goalkeeper)

Born: 18.8.68, London
Height: 6ft 1in
Weight: 12st 7lb
Signed for Celtic: August 1997 from Bradford City
Other league clubs: Halifax Town, West Bromwich Albion, Coventry City
Season record: 48 apps, 0 goals

Signed as cover for the injured Gordon Marshall and Stewart Kerr at the beginning of the season. Debuted in a friendly against Roma – when Marshall came down with a virus – and kept his place. Kept a clean sheet through the entire Coca-Cola Cup campaign.

Jackie McNamara (Defender)

Born: 24.10.73, Glasgow
Height: 5ft 9in
Weight: 10st 4lb
Signed for Celtic: October 1995 from Dunfermline
Other league clubs: None
Season record: 43 apps, 3 goals
Celtic career: 115 apps, 5 goals

The son of a former Celt, McNamara is one of the most exciting young players in the game and has easily stepped up a level since joining Celtic. Was used by Wim Jansen as a right-sided midfielder rather than a full-back. Was named Players' Player of the Year for 1997–98.

Tosh McKinlay (Defender)

Born: 3.12.69, Glasgow
Height: 5ft 8in
Weight: 11st 6lb
Signed for Celtic: November 1994 from Hearts
Other league clubs: Dundee
Season record: 10 apps, 0 goals
Celtic career: 113 apps, 0 goals

Came into his own when he joined his boyhood heroes in a surprise move. His no-nonsense defending coupled with his overlapping runs and crosses from the left, pushed him into the Scotland squad late in his career. Out of favour with Wim Jansen, but Craig Brown kept faith and took him to the World Cup in France.

Tom Boyd (Defender)

Born: 24.11.65, Glasgow
Height: 5ft 11in
Weight: 12st 10lb
Signed for Celtic: February 1992 from Chelsea
Other league clubs: Motherwell
Season record: 47 apps, 0 goals
Celtic career: 294 apps, 2 goals

Promoted to club captain following Paul McStay's retirement, Boyd is the model professional. A regular fixture for club and country he earned his fiftieth Scotland cap in 1997–98 and takes his place in the SFA Hall of Fame.

Stephane Mahé (Defender)

Born: 9.9.68, France
Height: 6ft
Weight: 11st 10lb
Signed for Celtic: August 1997 from Rennes

Other league clubs: Auxerre, Paris St-Germain

Season record: 35 apps, 1 goal

Played against Celtic for Paris St-Germain in the 1995–96 European Cup-Winners' Cup but then moved to Auxerre and then Rennes. Came to Scotland to revive his career and was first-choice left-back until a bad knee injury kept him out of the title run-in.

Alan Stubbs (Defender)

Born: 6.10.71, Lancashire

Height: 6ft 2in

Weight: 12st 12lb

Signed for Celtic: May 1996 from Bolton

Other league clubs: None

Season record: 42 apps, 2 goals

Celtic career: 68 apps, 3 goals

The club record signing had a difficult first season. Alongside Marc Rieper, Stubbs was outstanding in his second season and scored a vital equaliser against Rangers in the second Old Firm game.

Marc Rieper (Defender)

Born: 5.6.68, Denmark

Height: 6ft 4in

Weight: 14st 2lb

Signed for Celtic: September 1997 from West Ham

Other league clubs: FC Aarhus, Brondby

Season record: 36 apps, 3 goals

A Danish internationalist with more than 50 caps, Rieper settled in superbly to the defence at Celtic Park alongside Alan Stubbs. Scored the opening goal in the Coca-Cola Cup final.

Malky Mackay (Defender)

Born: 19.2.72, Lanarkshire
Height: 6ft
Weight: 13st 6lb
Signed for Celtic: August 1994 from Queen's Park
Other league clubs: None
Season record: 9 apps, 1 goal
Celtic career: 49 apps, 5 goals

The former bank worker has turned down moves to other clubs to fight for his place in the Celtic first-team squad. Scored the first goal of the season against Hibs, but since the arrival of Marc Rieper has found himself out of first-team plans and has since moved to Norwich City.

Enrico Annoni (Defender)

Born: 10.7.66, Italy
Height: 5ft 10in
Weight: 12st 9lb
Signed for Celtic: March 1997 from AS Roma
Other league clubs: Seregno, Como, Sambenedettese, Torino
Season record: 25 apps, 0 goals
Celtic career: 30 apps, 0 goals.

Celtic's Bald Eagle recovered from being out of Wim Jansen's plans, to establish himself as a regular towards the end of the season. A mean man-marker, his appearances have been restricted by injury, but he has become a cult figure among the Celtic support.

David Hannah (Midfielder/defender)

Born: 4.8.74, Lanarkshire
Height: 5ft 11in
Weight: 11st 11lb
Signed for Celtic: December 1996 from Dundee United
Other league clubs: None

Season record: 25 apps, 1 goal

Celtic career: 48 apps, 1 goal

Hannah was used sparingly in a utility role and filled in at right-back early in the season. A change in team formation, however, left him a squad member for much of the season.

Paul Lambert (Midfielder)

Born: 7.9.69, Glasgow

Height: 5ft 11in

Weight: 10st 10lb

Signed for Celtic: November 1997 from Borussia Dortmund

Other league clubs: St Mirren, Motherwell

Season record: 31 apps, 2 goals

Reborn midfielder who finished his football education during his European Cup-winning year at Dortmund after leaving Motherwell under the Bosman ruling. Fills a holding role at Celtic and seldom wastes a ball.

Phil O'Donnell (Midfielder)

Born: 23.3.72, Lanarkshire

Height: 5ft 11in

Weight: 11st 7lb

Signed for Celtic: September 1994 from Motherwell

Other league clubs: None

Season record: 22 apps, 2 goals

Celtic career: 99 apps, 16 goals

O'Donnell has consistently struggled with injury since his arrival at the club. Battled his way back to fitness to fill a vital role in the run-in to the title.

Simon Donnelly (Midfielder/forward)

Born: 1.12.74, Glasgow
Height: 5ft 9in
Weight: 10st 6lb
Signed for Celtic: July 1992 from Queen's Park BC
Other league clubs: None
Season record: 44 apps, 16 goals
Celtic career: 162 apps, 37 goals

Talented young star who had his best-ever season for Celtic in 1997–98 with 16 goals, despite spending time warming the subs bench. A versatile player, he can move from the centre to the right and vice versa.

Morten Wieghorst (Midfielder)

Born: 25.2.71, Denmark
Height: 6ft 3in
Weight: 13st
Signed for Celtic: December 1995 from Dundee
Other league clubs: Lyngby
Season record: 42 apps, 8 goals
Celtic career: 73 apps, 11 goals

Wieghorst had a poor first season at Celtic because of injury. In 1997–98 he was a revelation. He won a well-deserved Man of the Match award in the Coca-Cola Cup final and forced his way into the Danish World Cup squad.

Craig Burley (Midfielder)

Born: 24.9.71, Ayr
Height: 6ft 1in
Weight: 11st 7lb
Signed for Celtic: July 1997 from Chelsea
Other league clubs: None
Season record: 48 apps, 15 goals

The former Chelsea star was an inspired signing. His surging runs made him a virtual ever-present in the Celtic midfield and he scored a number of crucial goals in his impressive final tally of 15. Was named Football Writers' Player of the Year and scored for Scotland against Norway in the World Cup finals.

Regi Blinker (Midfielder)

Born: 2.6.69, Surinam
Height: 5ft 8in
Weight: 11st 7lb
Signed for Celtic: August 1997 from Sheffield Wednesday
Other league clubs: Den Bosch, Feyenoord
Season record: 23 apps, 2 goals

The Dutchman scored on his Celtic debut, but loss of form cost him his place mid-season. A wide man in the old-fashioned style Blinker made his first-team comeback at the end of the season.

Henrik Larsson (Forward)

Born: 10.9.71, Sweden
Height: 5ft 9in
Weight: 11st 2lb
Signed for Celtic: July 1997 from Feyenoord
Other league clubs: None
Season record: 47 apps, 19 goals

Lured from Feyenoord for a bargain price, Larsson became arguably the most influential player on the road to Celtic's championship. His 19 goals were vital and also earned him a recall to the Swedish international squad.

Darren Jackson (Forward)

Born: 25.7.66, Edinburgh

Height: 5ft 10in

Weight: 11st 11lb

Signed for Celtic: July 1997 from Hibernian

Other league clubs: Meadowbank Thistle, Newcastle United, Dundee
   United

Season record: 31 apps, 6 goals

The first signing of the season received a potential body blow to his
career when he required brain surgery just weeks into the season.
Recovered magnificently to play an important role in the championship
race and also forced his way back into Scotland's World Cup squad.

Harald Brattbakk (Forward)

Born: 1.2.71, Norway

Height: 5ft 10in

Weight: 11st

Signed for Celtic: December 1997 from Rosenborg

Other league clubs: Bodo

Season record: 21 apps, 10 goals

The lightning-quick Norwegian achieved an impressive strike record in
half a season at Celtic Park. Scored the goal which put Celtic 2–0 up
against St Johnstone and effectively clinched the first title in a decade.

Tommy Johnson (Forward)

Born: 15.1.71, Newcastle

Height: 5ft 11in

Weight: 12st 4lb

Signed for Celtic: April 1997 from Aston Villa

Other league clubs: None

Season record: 4 apps, 2 goals

Celtic career: 10 apps, 4 goals

Desperately unlucky with injuries and found it difficult to force his way into the squad.

John Paul McBride (Midfielder)

Born: 28.11.78, Lanarkshire
Height: 5ft 9ins
Weight: 10st
Signed for Celtic: August 1995 from Celtic Boys Club
Other league clubs: None
Season record: 1 app, 0 goals
Celtic career: 3 apps, 0 goals

One of the brightest young prospects in the game. Went to the same school as Paul McStay and Phil O'Donnell, so the pedigree seems sound. Made his sole appearance as a substitute against Inter CableTel.

The following players also took part in the championship campaign but left the club during the season.

Andreas Thom	24 apps	7 goals
Gordon Marshall	3 apps	0 goals
Stuart Gray	2 apps	0 goals
Chris Hay	1 app	1 goal
Peter Grant	1 app,	0 goals

APPENDIX C

The Championship Table

	P	W	D	L	F	A	Pts
Celtic	36	22	8	6	64	24	74
Rangers	36	21	9	6	76	38	72
Hearts	36	19	10	7	70	46	67
Kilmarnock	36	13	11	12	40	52	50
St Johnstone	36	13	9	14	38	42	48
Aberdeen	36	9	12	15	39	53	39
Dundee United	36	8	13	15	43	51	37
Dunfermline	36	8	13	15	43	68	37
Motherwell	36	9	7	20	46	64	34
Hibernian	36	6	12	18	38	59	30